Marketing in Developing Countries

Nigerian Advertising in a Global and Technological Economy

Emmanuel C. Alozie

Routledge
Taylor & Francis Group
New York   London

First published 2009
by Routledge
270 Madison Ave, New York, NY 10016

Simultaneously published in the UK
by Routledge
2 Park Square, Milton Park, Abingdon, Oxon OX14 4RN

Routledge is an imprint of the Taylor & Francis Group, an informa business

© 2009 Taylor & Francis

Typeset in Sabon by IBT Global.
Printed and bound in the United States of America on acid-free paper by IBT Global.

Library of Congress Cataloging-in-Publication Data
Alozie, Emmanuel C.
  Marketing in developing countries : Nigerian advertising in a global and technological economy / by Emmanuel C. Alozie.
    p. cm. — (Routledge studies in international business and the world economy)
  Includes bibliographical references and index.
  1. Advertising—Nigeria.   2. Mass media—Nigeria.   3. Marketing—Nigeria.
4. Advertising—Africa, Sub-Saharan.   5. Marketing—Africa, Sub-Saharan.   I. Title.
  HF5813.N55A464 2005
  658.8009669—dc22
  2008027809

ISBN10: 0-7890-0141-1 (hbk)
ISBN10: 0-203-88469-8 (ebk)

ISBN13: 978-0-7890-0141-2 (hbk)
ISBN13: 978-0-203-88469-0 (ebk)

In memory of my father who toiled and sacrificed for me but did not live to reap the fruit of his labor—"SP achieved the Golden Fleece". You remain my hero, the loving, the likable and unassuming man who cared for me and everyone you came across. To my mother for her continued prayers and sacrifice and bearing the absence of your only surviving child in your later years. To memories of my late brothers—Donatus, Polycarp and Kevin—"will you know me when you see me in heaven?"

Contents

Acknowledgments

I credit the publication of this book to my parents Boniface and Agatha NwAlozie-Amah who instilled in me the passion for education and for the guidance they offered that influenced my academic path and achievements. Without their insistence, this fruit would not have been borne. I am indebted to my wife Caroline for her support in every way—my cheer-in-chief. Special thanks goes to my sons, Nnanna, Emmanuel (for their editorial assistance), and Amechi-Chikwadolam Anthony for bearing my absence and temperament.

I owe a number of people a great deal of debt for my intellectual growth that helped me to bring this project to fruition. Academic debts are owed to Mazharul Haque, chair of my doctoral committee, for his thoughtful directions; Tommy V. Smith and other members of my doctoral committee at the University of Southern Mississippi. Academic debts are also owed to Pam Brock, Remigus Iheakam, Mrs. Nwankwo [my English Literature tutor, wife of my principal at Priscilla Memorial Grammar School (P.M.G.S.), Oguta]; Marlin Shipman, the late M.A.K. Akalonu, the late Dr. B.C. Njoku, and the late Dr. Robert Hoskins. Professional and personal debts are due to Mrs. A.E.T. Makinde, Dr. Roger Oden, Raphael Nwaiwu, Polycarp U. Okere, Gbolahan Olugbenga, Gregory Okere, Gorden Akaliso, Cosmas Nkwocha, Innocent Nkwocha, Debra Whitfield, Alfred J. Stovall, Fannie Lampley, and Steve Dunson.

I would like to acknowledge the institutions that contributed to my academic and professional growth. The Nigerians institutions are St. Thomas Church and Community School, Umuowa; P.M.G.S. Oguta; Holy Ghost College and Government College, Owerri; and United Bank for Africa, Lagos; while the American institutions include Rust College, Arkansas State University, the University of Southern Mississippi, Edward Waters College, Lincoln University, Shaw University, Governors State University, North Carolina A&T State University, Freedom Forum, American Society of Newspaper Editors Institute, Cap Cities/American Broadcasting Company, Inland Press Association, American Press Institute, Associated Press, United Negro College Fund, United Bank for Africa, *Oakland Tribune,*

Kansas City Star, Topeka Capital-Journal, Asbury Park Press, and St. Mary's Health Center, Jefferson City, Missouri.

To my friends, cohorts, academic colleagues, teachers, reviewers and students and formers teachers whose input I enjoyed as I worked on this book and other academic endeavors

1 Role of Marketing in Developing Countries

INTRODUCTION AND SIGNIFICANCE

The role of advertising in a market economy is to inform as well as educate consumers about products and services. To achieve these goals, advertisers employ a variety of values in their appeals. An *advertising appeal* may be defined as a creative attempt to motivate consumers toward some form of activity or influence attitude to make a product or service attractive or interesting to the consumer (Wells, Burnett, and Moriarty, 1992).

As a vehicle for promoting social modernization, the impact of utilizing advertising to promote consumerism in developing societies remains a subject of intense debate in this era of when globalization and development of information and communication technologies (ICTs) have brought the world closer. In an era of globalization and technological development, where the exchange of information travels rapidly, Roberts (1987) points out that the debate about the influence of advertising in most societies, especially developing nations, revolves around one primary issue: Do advertising messages reflect the cultural values of the developing and traditional societies within which they are communicated or do they seek to introduce Western values that reinforce the consumption habits of the capitalist-industrial world?

Critics allege that advertising relies on overwhelmingly persuasive and symbolic images to sell products and services by "associating them with certain socially desirable qualities, but they sell, as well, a world view, a life-style, and a value system congruent with the imperatives of consumer capitalism" (Kellner, 1988, p. 37). Activists in developing nations, supported by some Western scholars, claim this is especially true in developing countries, such as Nigeria, where multinational organizations depend on advertising to convey covert propaganda, thus circulating globally Western-made messages, imagery, lifestyle, and socioeconomic values at the expense of traditional ideas (Fejes, 1980; Janus, 1986; Schiller, 1979). Most of these countries do not have the resources to monitor the activities of the advertisers (Fejes, 1980; Janus, 1986; Schiller, 1979).

Past studies of cross-cultural advertising have dealt with the portrayal of gender roles in TV promotions, creative strategies, themes, information contents, execution, and humor in advertising (Ahmad, 1995; Cheng, 1997; Cheng & Schweitzer, 1996; Frith & Wesson, 1991; Mueller, 1987; Zandpour et al., 1994). Zandpour explains that these studies suggest that differences exist in advertising messages and appeals and that these differences are often assumed to reflect cultural variations. It may be argued that these studies have dealt with the interplay between advertising and cultural values both within and across cultures in the Information Age. They have been drawn and produced by the use of mechanistic and quantitative methods, such as content analysis at the expense of qualitative methods (Zandpour et al., 1994). At the same, past studies have hardly examined the role, relationship, and impact of advertising and information technologies on African societies as the current one intends to do (Al-Olayan, & Karande, 2000; Harris & Attour, 2000).

Considering the need to expand the knowledge of the role of advertising and its interplay with emerging information and communication technologies in the developing world, the purpose of this book is threefold:

1. The study uses political economy to investigate the connection among social modernization, socioeconomic development, and ICTs, considering that technological developments are viewed as vehicles for not only introducing, but also maintaining, values conveyed in mass media artifacts, which in turn exert some degree of that influence on a society. Technological determinism and globalization form the basis conceptual framework.
2. The study also uses qualitative analysis techniques (critical and cultural analyses) to ascertain the cultural values and ideas manifested in advertisements in Nigerian mass media advertising. When used to uncover the meaning hidden beneath mass media artifacts, cultural criticism provides an avenue for scholars to study cultures that have been oppressed socially, politically, economically, or militarily (Brummett, 1994).
3. Based on the findings, the study attempts to make suggestions and recommendations regarding the conduct and prospects of advertising in Nigeria and other African countries and its relationship with ICTs as well as the role of ICTs.

RESEARCH QUESTIONS

To achieve the objectives of this book, three primary research questions guide the conduct of this study:

1. What is the role, status, relationship, and impact of ICTs on advertising and the socioeconomic development of Nigeria and Sub-Saharan Africa?
2. What are the dominant cultural values and symbols conveyed in Nigerian mass media advertising?

3. What are the connotations and implications (positive and/or negative) of these values, ideas, signs, and symbols?

By exploring these specific questions, it is hoped that the study contributes to the debate about whether consumer advertising in the developing relies on traditional or Western values and cultures as elements of persuasion. In doing so, the study also attempts to determine whether advertising contributes to or distorts the socioeconomic development of Nigeria and other Third World countries in an increasingly global economy as proponents on either side of the debate contend.

The findings of this research arm foreign investors, government officials, corporations, and entrepreneurs with the essential information about the African marketplace, African consumers, and the business and technological environments to empower them to make informed and wise decisions as they invest in Africa. The findings of the study may help African governments as well as indigenous and international businesses in Africa and other parts of the Third World to develop advertising messages that are culturally sensitive and effective. Understanding the prevailing cultural, socioeconomic, and technological evolution in an emerging economy may enable investors, manufacturers, and marketers to create culturally sensitive advertising messages that may assist and not distort the economic development of Third World nations.

Finally, another goal of this study is to present the status of information and communication technologies in Nigeria and other African countries and their intersection with advertising and economic development. It is hoped that the findings prepare existing investors and businesses entities and those entering the Nigerian economy to understand the challenges they may encounter regarding the conduct of business and the acquisition and use of ICTs. Also, the study offers information and strategies regarding plans for effective investments in new technologies in developing nations. Effective development of ICTs and their proper use in marketing and socioeconomic activities will assist the economic development of Nigeria and other societies in Africa and the Third World.

WHY STUDY ADVERTISING IN NIGERIA AND AFRICA?

During his first visit to Africa in 1998, President Bill Clinton shunned Nigeria, one of America's largest trading partners. He avoided the continent's most populous and natural resource-rich nation because the international community accused the military administration of General Sani Abacha, which governed the nation military, of violating human rights, curtailing freedom, and mismanaging the economy. The Abacha administration's policies made Nigeria an international pariah. After Abacha's death in June 1998, reportedly of a heart attack, the military junta selected Major

General Abdulsalam Abubakar as head of state. Bowing to domestic and international pressures to restore democracy, Abubakar conducted general elections, in which General Olusegun Obasanjo, a former military head, was elected president.

More than a year after Nigeria returned to democratic rule under Olusegun Obasanjo in May 1999, Clinton embarked on a 3-day symbolic visit to the country in August 2000 accompanied by prominent African Americans, American politicians, entrepreneurs, and corporate leaders. The president's visit demonstrated Nigeria's potentials as a prospective leading economy and evolution of political pluralism in Africa and the Third World, as well as an important player in the technological and global economy. Clinton called on Nigeria, described as Africa's sleeping giant, to awaken from her slumber if she is to realize her political, economic, and scientific promises and drive the coming African renaissance. He stated that the success of Nigeria's political and economic reforms would serve as an example for other African nations (*Vanguard*, 2000, Aug. 28). Clinton was implying that if Africa is to fully benefit from emerging worldwide political pluralism (Newsom, 2004) and world trade that has grown from $200 billion to $4 trillion over the quarter of a year (Mueller, 1996), Nigeria must lead.

With a population of 127 million, Nigeria ranks as the 10th most populous nation in the world (*The Guardian Online*, 2001, Aug. 13). Barring wars, political disintegration, and social upheavals, Nigeria's population will surge to 204 million by 2025, thereby making it the world's seventh most populous nation. By 2050, the population will soar to 337 million to become the fourth most populated country in the world while India, China, and the United States will be the top three (Eribo, 2001). Thus, Nigeria promises to be a huge world marketplace in the near future. Endowed with a wealth of human and natural resources, Nigeria is one of the most industrialized African countries, with more than 2,000 industrial establishments. In an increasingly technological world, Nigeria, combined with the other 52 African nations, has the potential to become a golden arena for trade, commerce, and political plurality in the twenty-first century, comparable to India and China.

If Nigeria is to fulfill the goal that Clinton outlined, Nwosu (1990) contends that advertising must play a significant role. Okechukwu Onyia, managing director and chief executive of Concept Advertising, a mid-size Nigerian agency, said advertising is involved in most aspects of modern life. He states:

> It promotes the government, promotes the people who are seeking government positions, it promotes ideas and products and economy generally, in the rest of the world; it is through advertising that government can promote the economy of Nigeria. The stability of the economy, the stability of the polity and ability to say to investors out there, come,

we have a very viable economy, a producing economy and a very stable polity for you to come and invest and do business peacefully. It is through advertising that you can create this awareness in the international world. . . . (Amuzuo, 2000b)

He adds that marketing and promotions are relevant to governance and socioeconomic development in Nigeria. Onyia said that integrating advertising and public relations could serve as a marketing tool geared toward promoting ideas, concepts, and programs. Distinguishing between advertising and public relations, he explains the former promotes products, services, and corporate bodies, whereas the latter promotes people, corporate bodies, government, and ideas. Advertorials serve a public relations role as well. He states that marketing:

> Will play a lot of role in the emerging civil economy in Nigeria because if you look elsewhere like the United States, advertising has permeated all aspects of life. Anything you do in America revolves around promotions. You promote yourself, you promote your corporate body, you promote your product, you promote your family. . . . (Amuzuo, 2000b)

It should be noted that studies regarding the role of advertising in international trade and the socioeconomic development of nations have been on the rise for the past 50 years (Pollay & Gallagher, 1990). The interest could be attributed to the recognition that advertising is an effective and persuasive medium for educating and informing the public about products, services, and ideas; it is also a driving tool for changing beliefs, attitudes, and behaviors (Sandage, 1990). Within this time frame, ICTs and globalization have transformed the world into a single large marketplace (Sussman, 1997), but a marketplace where economic philosophies and cultural value differences exist (Cheng, 1997). In an increasingly technological and global world, few have examined the relationship and role of various forms of advertising, as well as the impact of evolving technological changes in Africa as this study intends to accomplish (Cheng, 1997; Lin, 2001; Stafford, 2005; Zandpour et al., 1994).

To communicate effectively with consumers in a specific society, advertisers have realized the need to examine and understand sociocultural distinctions in a country (Keegan, 1989). This recognition has compelled advertisers and marketers to place emphasis on intercultural communication because it is generally accepted that consumers have favorable attitudes toward messages that reflect their own sociocultural values. Moreover, consumers reward advertisers that understand their cultures and tailor their messages to reflect those values (Boddewyn, Soehl, & Picard, 1986). Studies show that international businesses that recognize the cultures and social conditions of host nations and use marketing appeals and strategies that reflect a society's cultural values reduce misunderstandings and mistrust between consumers marketers (Wells, 1994).

Although there has been a wealth of intercultural studies on advertising for almost half a century, few scholars have examined the information or cultural content in any African country (Abernethy, Franke, & George, 1996; Al-Olayan & Karande, 2000; Harris & Attour, 2000). This remains a shortcoming that Al-Olayan and Karande (2000) attempted to change by exploring the cultural content of advertising in mass media in the Middle East and 10 African countries (Algeria, Egypt, Eritrea, Djibouti, Libya, Mauritania, Morocco, Somalia, Sudan, and Tunisia). However, this study concentrates primarily on North African nations with predominant Muslim and Arab cultures. Its findings cannot be generalized to Sub-Saharan Africa. Sudan, Somalia, and Eritrea are considered as the only Sub-Saharan African countries in the study. The failure to include more Sub-Saharan African nations, particularly those not dominated by Muslim cultures, as well as the continent's economic giants such as Nigeria and South Africa, calls for more studies to bridge the continued gap (CNN.com, 2001, Jan. 25; *Vanguard*, 2000, Aug. 28).

Foreign and indigenous corporations operating in Africa and organizations hoping to invest in the continent do not have resources that will enable them to tailor their messages toward African consumers because of the lack of advertising research in Africa. They also lack adequate information about the economic and political conditions in African countries, which leads to misconception. Prospective investors rely on information, techniques, and messages developed outside the continent. Dependence on information provided by western scholars and journalists (recorders in a hurry), who do not understand or have adequate knowledge of the continent, contributes to lack of interest, misconceptions, and business failures. This failure contributes to the ongoing debate in Africa that advertising promotes cultural imperialism and dependency while paralyzing the economic development of African as well as other developing nations (LaPalombra, 1979).

Considering Nigeria's socioeconomic status as a leading economic nation in the Third World, the importance attached to advertising, and the acquisition of ICTs in Nigeria to promote modernization in this era of globalization, the purpose of this study is to explore and determine the particular cultural values and symbols conveyed in Nigerian mass media advertising. Moreover, it addresses the debate regarding the role of ICTs as vehicles for introducing and maintaining the impact of advertising in the developing world.

The current exploration is important because, despite the interest in international and intercultural studies on advertising and the role of ICTs in an interconnected world economy, these subjects remain underresearched in Nigeria and other African nations. Viewed as the next economic frontier of the new millennium, it is important to encourage market research and publication on advertising, social conditions, and technological development in

Africa. Most of these studies have not involved the role of ICTs. Herbig and Miller (1992) contend that social changes emanate from the adoption of any and all new technologies. This contention demonstrates that ICTs play significant roles in human development. The powerful influence of technology in socioeconomic development of mankind makes it an important subject to study.

Thus, as indicated earlier, political economy will explore the relationship among technology, advertising, culture, and economic development in an era when the adoption of ICTs continues to play a wide range of roles on human and societal developments, especially the Third World's (Woods, 1993). The rationale of exploring a discussion of ICTs is to: (a) discern the status of African countries regarding acquiring information and communication technologies, (b) examine their role as a vehicle for conveying advertisements and media artifacts and the cultural impact, (c) investigate their impact in national and global marketing, and (d) suggest how a country such as Nigeria or others in the continent should proceed in acquiring ICTs.

As stated earlier, it is assumed such will offer some understanding of the role of advertising as a propaganda tool and its ability to influence mass culture in a technologically driven world. With little attention paid to the status of technology in Africa and its influence conveying mass media artifacts such as advertising, emphasis is placed on their interactions in a global economy that has become increasingly reliant on ICTs. Historically, technology has always paved the way for exploiting Africa (Mendelssohn, 1976). This exploitation creates the need to examine the role of ICTs in contemporary African society to ensure that they play positive, not destructive, roles because of their economic impact and ability to convey mass media artifacts. They also serve the primary vehicles for relaying advertising worldwide.

ORIGIN OF ADVERTISING

Advertising has existed since antiquity. The Bible and other ancient historical documents have demonstrated that advertising represented an avenue for disseminating information in a limited scope to small groups. In ancient times, Athens, Egypt, and Rome relied on signs and symbols displayed on shops to promote the goods and services provided. Signs and symbols were placed on buildings, walls, and rocks to provide news about events, goods, and services to small communities. Town criers were also used to spread information. This art of advertising began in ancient times, and, to date, it remains a significant means of declaiming information in developing countries. Town criers walk through public places, making stops at strategic locations to make announcements (Pasqua, Buckalew, Rayfied, & Tankard, 1990).

These ancient forms of advertising began to change with the invention of moveable type in the fifteenth century. Advertising evolved into recognizable forms such as handbills and posters to relay information to a larger audience.

Although the reach of advertising expanded, it remained a limited medium for relaying information because it reached a limited group at one time. Roberts (1987) points out that "mass advertising has not always been with us. It grew with mass media, or rather mass media grew with it" (p. 270).

THE ADVERTISING CONTROVERSY AND EMERGING ECONOMIES

Since the inception of mass media advertising, Roberts (1987) contends that advertising has been at the center of a continuing controversy or a series of controversies regarding its ethics, standards, and role in societies. This debate (Roberts, 1987) revolves around four questions: (a) Do the benefits of advertising outweigh its negative effects? (b) Should society really be concerned about the potential and actual abuses of advertising? (c) Does society really influence advertising? (d) If so, how much?

As Roberts (1987) contends, the relationship among promotional communication (commercial advertising, advertorials, and public relations), ICTs, cultural values, control, and economic development remains multidimensional (Newsom, 2004). This complex relationship requires continued research inquiry in an era when emerging democratic and capitalistic societies in Africa, Asia, and South America are increasingly relying on advertising and communication technologies as tools to promote economic, economic, and political development.

Areas of inquiry include values conveyed in advertising, messages conveyed in political advertising, and the role of information and communication in neoliberal environments where few entities and elites exert extensive control over the masses. Areas of inquiry include the role of ICTs in neoliberal environments of the postmodern era, in which few entities and elites them exert extensive control over the masses through values conveyed in advertising and messages conveyed in political communication.

Despite this need, there has been a paucity of research on the role of advertising in Nigeria and other countries in Africa (Abernethy, Franke, & George, 1996; Al-Olayan & Karande, 2000; Harris & Attour, 2000). If entities concerned with socioeconomic development in the region are to be made aware of the usefulness of advertising as a vehicle for the development of the economy and how to employ communication strategies to promote their programs, Nwosu (1990) urged scholars to conduct more studies on marketing to gain knowledge. Doing so will provide practitioners with the information needed to develop and tailor their messages and strategies effectively.

Tunde Ojo, managing director and chief executive of Lagos, Nigeria-based Touchstone Marketing Communications Limited, agrees. Citing the Nigerian banking industry, he said many Nigerian banks collapsed because they were not adequately packaged and presented by marketing practitioners who moved from promotional practices in manufacturing to the service sector. These marketing practitioners did not realize "the way you package your service is likely different from the way you package consumer products, because the marketing of services is largely different from the marketing of consumer products" (*Vanguard*, 1999, Nov. 11). This could be attributed to the fact that marketing practitioners lack adequate resources to enhance their knowledge on marketing in Sub-Saharan Africa resulting from a lack of research. This is one of the gulfs this study intends to bridge.

Describing advertising as one of the most perceptible activities of business, Arens (2004) states that advertising receives both praise and condemnation for the role the medium plays in selling products, services, and idea and influencing society with regard to its economic and social functions on individuals and a societies. As an economic activity, Arens likened advertising to an opening short in billiards that produces a chain reaction that affects an enterprise as well as its competitors, customers, and the business community. The reaction, he claims, triggers a national mass-distribution system, allowing manufacturers to produces the goods and services that people want in large volume, at a low price, with standardized quality. He observes that in developed economies, where there is an overproduction of products and services, advertising offers consumers complete information about products and services and choices available to them. The medium encourages manufacturers and providers to compete intensively, thus serving the self-interest of the marketers and consumers.

However, Arens (2004) points out that critics question "how advertising adds values to products, affects prices, encourages or discourages competition, promotes consumer demand, narrows or widens consumers choice, and affects business cycles" (p. 93). These concerns loom large in deprived economies of developing nations, where the social impact of advertising has been a subject contention. Critics argue that advertising is deceptive, manipulates people into buying unneeded goods and services, and forces people to engage in materialistic pursuits. Advertising is also blamed for promoting stereotypes, undermining cultural values, and enhancing materialism, and it remains offensive (Arens, 2004; Pollay & Gallagher, 1990). It may be added that in developing countries advertising contributes to corruption because those in position of responsibility engage in illegal activity to acquire money to purchase goods they have been exposed to through media and information technologies.

Thus, as a vehicle for promoting social modernization in an interlocked global economy, the impact of utilizing advertising continues to provoke intense examination. Roberts (1987) states that opinion leaders in developing countries blame advertising for undermining traditional values and economies in their societies while promoting Western capitalism values and consumption tendencies.

However, advocates of advertising argue that advertising is a powerful vehicle for economic development because it promotes mass marketing and mass production of goods and services. Schudson (1984) described the dominant role advertising plays in Western system as "capitalist realism." Advocates of advertising also argue that advertisers tailor their messages to cultivate modern habits and disseminate divergent values and ideas to promote the welfare of individuals and businesses (Kirkpatrick, 1990; Mueller, 1996; Schudson, 1984). They also claim that governments, organizations, and individuals can use advertising to relay political, economic, and social information to the public (Amuzuo, 2000b).

Conversely, critics of advertising contend that the medium promotes a consumerist society in undeveloped economies and undermines the cultural values of Third World countries. By promoting consumerism and undermining their culture, critics claim that advertising is detrimental to the socioeconomic and political stability of developing countries (Anderson, 1984; Mueller, 1996). Critics contend that ICTs increase the influence of mass media artifacts such as advertising because consumers can be reached in the most remote parts of the world (Mowlana, 1996; Sussman, 1997). Critics also argue that elites in a society use mass media including advertising as instruments to hold on to power, impose their values, and promote their interests (Lorimer & Gahser, 2001).

However, moderates point out that both of these contentions are too simplistic. Considering that every society has its own unique sociocultural history and values, moderates argue that an understanding of the role that advertising plays in the socioeconomic development of a specific nation must be discerned from the context of a particular society. Noting that advertising champions a consumer culture, unleashes untold expectations for the masses, and spurs sub-Saharan African elites to depend on imported goods, Domatob (1987) points out that advertising fosters the development of underdeveloped societies. It encourages the development of new products and services, gives businesses and consumers a variety of choices, and stimulates competition. It fosters employment, encourages mass production, keeps prices down, and raises the standard of living (Arens, 2004). Advertising serves as a source of many aspects of information. Nwosu (1990) agrees. He contends that advertising can be used to promote desirable social aims such as savings, investments, family planning, and the purchase of fertilizer to improve agricultural production (Domatob, 1987). Both scholars agree that advertising serves as a source of information about possible patterns of expenditure regarding personal needs, in-house purchases, and rental and travel services.

MARKETING, COMMUNICATION DEVELOPMENT, AND NATIONAL TRANSFORMATION

African administrations and other governments in the developing world acknowledge the role of mass communications in national development. These governments recognized, invested, and developed their mass media

and telecommunications infrastructures as vehicles to be used for the political, economic, cultural, and social mobilization as well as the modernization and development of their countries and their peoples (Bourgault,
1995; Faringer, 1991). Moemeka (1994) describes the policy as communication development, which these governments hoped would enable them to
implement development communication. The use of mass communication
channels as vehicles for social mobilization and transformation is called
development communication/journalism.

Ngugi (1995) pointed out that the concept was conceived as a means of
facilitating development by "systematic utilization of appropriate communication channels and techniques to increase people's participation in development
and to inform, motivate and train rural populations mainly at the grassroots
levels" (p. 7). Encouraged by Western institutions and transnational corporations, advertising remains one of the channels that Third World governments
have relied on to promote national development. *National development* is
defined as an effort to enhance the human, cultural, socioeconomic, and
political conditions of the individual and society (Moemeka, 1994). It refers
to the process of integrating the masses to cultivate a national identity, encouraging mass participation in the planning process, and promoting an equitable
distribution of economic benefits. It encourages and permits the penetration
and provision of effective social services at all levels of a society.

However, Nwosu (1990) states that Nigerian and other African governments disregarded advertising and public relations as a medium for promoting their policies or providing information to people on a variety of issues
concerning national development. He attributed that neglect to the lack of
awareness of governments and organizations in sub-Saharan Africa about
the usefulness of government advertising. In this regard, Chris Doghudje, a
Nigerian advertising manager, contends that:

> It is now a fact universally acknowledged that the most powerful means
> by which the availability of goods and services can be known is adver-
> tising. This is why capitalist countries embrace advertising. But not
> everybody is aware that advertising is also the most powerful means for
> the selling of ideas, of policies and of government. Too often advertis-
> ing is seen as no more than a selling tool to be used by businessmen. But
> governments, charitable organizations, and political parties all need
> advertising for the promotion of their ideas, policies and worthwhile
> causes. (Domatob, 1987, p. 285)

THE GLOBAL MARKET PLACE: ROLE OF ICTS

Technological progress that gave birth to the Industrial Revolution influenced the growth of modern advertising. In the mid-1800s, as the Industrial Revolution transformed Western economies from rural-agricultural

into big urban-industrialized societies, the production of goods and services grew exponentially. The mass production of goods and services created the need to find a wider market to dispose of them.

During this period, several factors changed the lives of millions of people. These included: increased literacy, the growth of print media, the movement from rural to urban areas, the mass demand for goods and services, and the possession of disposable income as a result of improved economic and social welfare. As living standards improved, there was an increase in the quest for information about available goods and services. In addition, the need for manufacturers to relay this information to consumers grew. Advertising began to fill the void, thus evolving from a limited to a mass medium. Technological improvements in print and other forms of communication, including transportation, influenced the growth of mass advertising. As the twenty-first century begins, rapid progress in ICTs still influence the reach of advertising to the global community.

The expansion of Western capitalism in the nineteenth and twentieth centuries could not have been possible without the use of ICTs to create a global communication infrastructure (Thussu, 2000). He notes that at the end of World War II, Western nations, led by United States of America's hegemony, used "soft power" to supplement military supremacy. Thussu points out that much of the Cold War was fought over the airwaves in the North. However, in the South, the war remained hot often. More than 20 million lives were claimed in conflicts between capitalism and communism for global domination. These deaths occurred mostly in the developing world.

In the post-Cold War era, TV and other forms of mass media's reach across borders have become conduits for conveying and legitimizing the free market ideology, which is dominated by corporate capitalism. Thussu (2000) explains that the new form of capitalism is distinguished from its colonial predecessor by its emphasis on the almost mythical powers and promises of the market; it is also distinguished by its use of mediated entertainment rather than coercion to propagate this message and values. Advertising serves as a primary vehicle for relaying as well as planting Western free marketing and sociocultural values in emerging societies. Having realized the power of advertising, the political and economic elites in Nigeria and other developing nations employ this as an instrument to sway the public (Boafo, 1985; Taylor, 2000).

WESTERN DOMINANCE OF INTERNATIONAL COMMUNICATIONS

The end of World War II marked the emergence of many new states in Africa and Asia. The rise of these countries created the need to improve the economic and social welfare of the people. Assisted by the political hegemony of the United States, several Western global corporations, including those from Japan, were presented with the opportunity to expand their operations or move into these newly independent states (Solomon, 1978). Global corporations depended on public relations, marketing, and advertising to extend their reach and to promote their growth and profitability by promoting their goods and services in these emerging countries (Sauvant, 1976; Schiller, 1977; Sreberny-Mohammadi, 1997).

However, the newly independent states relied on traditional forms of mass communication (broadcast and print), as well as public relations and advertising, as vehicles to promote economic development. Yet at the time of independence, most of these emerging states, including Nigeria, did not possess adequate technologies or the financial means to establish viable indigenous broadcasting, print, public relations, and advertising media agencies (Hamelink, 1997). Countries that did possessed operations either too unsophisticated or inadequate to compete with Western mass media outlets (Janus, 1980,1981; Ostheimer, 1973). As a result, the global corporations operating in the developing countries depended on Western advertising agencies to promote their products and services. That dependence gave Western Transnational Advertising Agencies a foothold in these countries. It enabled multinational corporations and Western transnational agencies to use Western-oriented advertising to dominate the market and mass media in developing nations (Anderson, 1984; Janus, 1980, 1981; Sauvant, 1976; Smith, 1980).

Thussu (2000) observes that for more than 100 years, the recurring theme in international communication has been the continued domination of the global information and entertainment industries (both hardware and software) by a few mainly Western nations and the transnational corporations. He explains that from Marconi to Microsoft, continuity can be detected regarding how mainly Western technology creates and sets the agenda of international communication, whether it is cabling the world, broadcasting to an international audience, or generating a virtual globe through the Internet.

Thus, mass media outlets and consumers, as well as governments in developing countries, have been and are becoming increasingly reliant on Western mass media for information and entertainment in this era of globalization (Uche, 1988, 1994, 1997). Even when programming comes from local sources, it is weighted with Western values. This is because Western corporations are the source of revenue for the always financially strapped mass media in the developing world (Fortner, 1993). Domatob (1988) describes this tendency as "neo-colonialism," which emanates from the economic and technical superiority of one group over the other. It should be noted that Africans have never viewed their cultural values as inferior to those of the West (Clarke, 1995; Oladipo, 1995).

Western organizations have been accused of undermining the growth and development of African and Third World mass media as well as political, social, cultural, and economic institutions. These organizations include multinational corporations, mass media organizations, and transnational advertising and public relations agencies. They are dominant in developing nations because of their superior technical, organizational, political, financial, and professional skills and their economic production capabilities (Anderson, 1984; Schiller, 1977, 1979; Smith, 1980; Tsao, 1996). In most Third World countries, the mass media depend on multinationals operating in their countries for revenue, which primarily originates from advertising and sponsorship.

Thussu (2000) expresses concerns about the flow of information and the world economic system in this globalization era in which most of the world is pursuing the dominant ideology of the West. This pursuit is influenced by major powers through their control of international channels of communication—telegraph, radio, TV, and the Internet. While acknowledging the dominance of Western media outlets with regard to content, flow of information, control of communication, and ability to influence impact on values, McChesney (2001) argues that dominance does not represent Western imperialism. Rather, he argues that neoliberal media system work in favor of few corporate media owners through the globalization of corporate and commercial values. He supports his view by asserting that Brazil's Globo and Mexico's Televisa are among the second tier of 40 to 50 regional media outlets that have become powerful because of penetration outside their countries of origin. He points out that as these outlets became successful, they have become increasingly advocates of procapitalist and liberal values (Grosswiler, 2004).

ORGANIZATION OF BOOK

Having discussed the role of advertising and information technologies in developing societies in this chapter, the organizational framework of the rest of this book is as follows:

Chapter 2 provides a brief history of Nigeria as well as examines the political economy of Nigeria and the African continent. Chapter 3 discusses Nigeria's advertising industry and sectors of mass media.

Chapter 4 reviews studies related to the continuing debate on the functions of advertising, cultural imperialism, and the convergence and impact of technology. Chapter 5 uses technological and cultural theories as its conceptual grounding to explore the connection between of advertising and ICTs. Chapter 6 uses political economy to explore the status of ICTs in Africa while ascertaining what is absent from the debate dealing with the role of technology in advertising, the impact of globalization, the digital divide, and the influence of technology in the developing world. The chapter highlights various theories on technology and also discusses the impact of information and communication technologies in advertising. It proposes a model that African nations should adopt in their quest to acquire ICTs. Chapter 7 employs textual analysis to explore the cultural values manifested in Nigerian mass media advertising. Chapter 8 provides a brief summary and conclusion of the study. Also, it discusses the major implications of the findings and recommendations for further studies.

2 Stages of Socioeconomic Development in Sub-Saharan Africa

IN SEARCH OF AFRICAN RESOURCES

European imperialism in Africa began when Magellan's ship concluded the circumnavigation of the earth almost a century after Prince Henry the Navigator of Portugal started and successfully organized a series of African expeditions in 1814. This successful exploration allowed trade to flourish on high seas instead of overland routes, which were often subject to robberies, demands for tributes, and other uncertainties. Ocean travel using large ships enabled the Europeans to move people in greater numbers, expand the amount of trade goods as well as routes, and establish many naval and trade points along the African coast.

Europeans settled in these bases. The bases were fortified and defended for white settlers by the Portuguese military (Mendelssohn, 1976). Having secured reliable trade routes and bases along African and Asian coasts, the Portuguese began to assume an imperialist posture. Using their superior scientific methods and military arms, the Portuguese imposed trade on their own terms. "The races with whom they traded soon ceased to be treated as equals: they began to be dominated, and this domination was to be gained by a conscious exploitation of the forces of nature" (Mendelssohn, 1976, p. 23). It marked the beginning of white domination over other races of the world that exists to date. These early contacts have been blamed for the dislocation of Africans and the destabilization of African political, social, and economic institutions.

Rodney (1974) argues that Africa's current political upheaval and economic underdevelopment could be traced to European policies. He contends that Africans were exploited for the benefit of European colonial powers. Although the colonial masters used cheap African labor to extract its resources, most of those resources were bundled out of the continent to the West, where they were processed into manufactured goods for world commerce and as exports to Africa at high prices (Mazrui, 1995). However, Agbango (1997) did absolve African leaders of their failures. He said that almost a half century after independence, most African countries suffer from chronic economic stagnation and underdevelopment, poverty, political instability, and health deprivation because of an ineptness of African leaders who have failed to improve the social welfare of the people (Mazrui, 1995). In recent years, African leaders have begun to look inward as well as outward to tackle the overwhelming problems that plague the continent (CNN.com, 2001, Jan. 25; Gaile & Ferguson, 1996).

During the 2001 World Economic Forum in Davos, Switzerland, South African President Thabo Mbeki used his address to call for support for a homegrown African Marshall Plan. He said the plan would serve as a vehicle for Africa to escape the conflict and poverty that holds the continent back while lending assistance for the continent to break away from its dependence on foreign aid and loans. He said the plan would help the continent find its place in the global marketplace on its own merit (CNN.com, 2001, Jan. 25).

According to the Debt Crisis Network, every man, woman, and child in sub-Saharan Africa now owes 250 pounds ($376) to rich creditors in developed countries. This may be a week's wage for many British citizens, but more than most Africans earn in a year. In 1995, African countries, some of the poorest in the world, paid 6 billion pounds ($9 billion) in debt repayments to their creditors (Logie, 1996).

The lack of Western investment in Nigeria and other African nations could be attributed to the fact that Africa is considered an economically "backward continent." Adam (1996) said that news coming out Africa is replete with the seven Ds (demography, desertification, drought, dependency, disequilibrium, debt, and destabilization), while Hawk (1992) adds that African political news deals with military coups, wars, corruption, violence, and AIDS policies. These negative-oriented stories camouflage the economic strength of Africa and the work achieved in the continent over the last decade.

Africa has a population of more than 700 million people. This number of potential consumers is expected to keep growing. Gaile and Ferguson (1996) state that the major indicators of social development in Africa are improving. Africans are working on ways to harness their natural and human resources into operative models of development. Africans are searching for their own paths to progress. They are acquiring limited prosperity and security. The rate of inflation is declining. Currencies are stabilizing due to compliance with stringent reform measures imposed by the International Monetary Fund (IMF) and other international financial institutions (McGeary & Michaels, 1998). It should be noted that these strict rules imposed on Africa by the IMF and World Bank for loaning money to African nations has been a source of criticism. Critics argue that the measures are harmful to Third World countries and contribute to the displacement of workers.

In recognition of these positive societal developments, the United Nations has earmarked $25 billion as part of its Special Initiative for Africa to assist and promote the continent's economic development (*Lancet*, 1997). The World Bank has called for increased domestic and private sector investments in Africa to complement greater trade liberalization, increased efforts to discourage corruption, economic and political reforms, and a solid legal framework within which businesses may operate that take place on the continent (*The Guardian*, 1999, May 11).

The introduction and passage of the Africa Trade and Opportunity Act during the Clinton administration demonstrates the recognition of the American government that an African renaissance has begun. The bill promotes trade between the United States and Africa. It is expected to start yielding dividends as American and Western investments continue to grow.

PERSPECTIVES ON NIGERIA

Historical

Nigeria has an ancient history dating back to 700 BC, with its diverse ethnic groups possessing their own unique rules, values, and beliefs that characterize their distinct cultural heritages (Associated Press, 1993, July 9; Olaniran & Roach, 1994).

Beginning in the mid-1800s, three events occurred that influenced the destiny and lives of diverse ethnic groups: Muslim warriors defeated ethnic groups in Northern Nigeria and imposed Islamic religion and culture, the Trans-Atlantic slavery trade was abolished, and early missionary activities in the field of modern education began (Embassy of Nigeria, 1998). In the late 1800s, Islam and Christianity clashed when missionaries and colonizers arrived on the continent.

During the European scramble and partition of Africa that intensified in the 1800s, the area that defined Nigeria came under the British sphere of influence. Britain established its colonial rule with the amalgamation of Southern and Northern Nigeria in 1914 (*Sunday Vanguard*, 2000).

Political

Describing the amalgamation and creation of Nigeria as a "fraud" perpetrated for the imperialist interest of Britain, Richard Akinjide, who served as a former minister of education and justice, under various administrations, blamed Britain for favoring the North over the South in political and economic matters during the colonial era (*Sunday Vanguard*, 2000). Nigeria gained independence from Britain in 1960. The Christian minority in Northern Nigeria blamed the Muslims for dictating to them through sultanates, caliphates, and emirates used by the British to maintain authority (Associated Press, 1993, July 9).

After gaining independence, rivalries and ethnic divisions that were submerged during the colonial era came to the fore. To date, conflicts instigated by politics in the West African nation are common and more deadly (Associated Press, 1993, July 9). In 1967, the Ibo-dominated southeast seceded, creating the nation of Biafra. A 3-year war ensued, in which from 250,000 to 1 million people [mostly Igbos] were killed or died of starvation (Associated Press, 1993, July 9).

Since independence in 1960, Nigeria has experienced a dozen years of democratic administration. Major-General Ishola Williams (rtd), former commander of the Training and Doctrine Command, identified the pitfalls of Nigerian politics and the democratization process. He placed the blame on a lack of integrity, accountability, transparency, contractocracy, and the militarized mindset of the civil society (Aja, 1998).

For more than 40 years of Nigerian nationhood, mainly Northern military officers have ruled the nation. Corruption, tribalism, political conflicts, and poor administration have been blamed for the failure of this nation, which is naturally abundant in mineral resources, to achieve its economic promise. Ethnic and religious differences, combined with economic woes, have caused instability in the country (Akinterinwa, 2001). Nigeria earns more than 90 percent of its income from oil.

Declaring the preconditions for the survival of the Nigerian experiment, if Nigeria is to help usher in the African renaissance of the twenty-first century, former head of state Chief Ernest Shonekan states that Nigeria must engage in good governance that encourages:

> the existence of political parties cutting across ethnic, religious and social lines; free responsible media; a professional military under the control of civil authorities; a generally accepted constitution defining the modus operandi of the citizens; and honest, hardworking politicians who believe in and can go to any length to defend the corporate existence of the country. (Anyigor, 1998, p. 1)

On May 29, 2007, when former President Olusegun Obasanjo handed over the reign of government to Umaru Yar'Adua, it marked the first time one civilian government handed power to another in 47 years of independence (Odili, 2007). The presidential, gubernatorial, and legislative elections were plagued with irregularities and are being disputed by several candidates and major political parties at election tribunals and courts (Collins, 2007). Obansanjo and Yar'Adua belong to the powerful Peoples Democratic Party that came to power in 1999. Obasanjo has described the irregularities that plagued the elections as "hiccups and problems" in the nation's democratic development (Amaizu, 2007). The former president has called on Nigerians to accept the shortcomings in the elections and transition as a leap forward for Nigerian democracy (CNN International.com, 2007, April 25).

Economic

Endowed with abundant natural and human resources, Nigeria contradicts the widely held belief that a nation's large population is a potentially inestimable asset that should bring cheers as a source for socioeconomic development, but judging from Nigeria's performance since gaining independence in modern times, the country faces a great hurdle (Lexis-Nexis, 2001; *The Guardian Online,* 2001, Aug. 13). Nigeria's population stands at 127 million. The World Population Data Sheet, which ranks the 60 top countries, rates Nigeria the 10th most populous nation in the world. The report adds that, by 2025, Nigeria's population will surge to 204 million, thereby positioning it as the world's seventh most populous country. About 25 years later (2025), the country's population will shoot up to become the sixth most populous nation with 303.5 million people (*The Guardian Online,* 2001, Aug. 13).

The nation's annual budget stands between $15 and $20 billion annually. Nigeria has earned more than $250 billion in oil windfalls from the time of her independence in 1960 through 1997 (Enyinnaya, 1998), but owed $30 to $35 billion to foreign organizations dating back to the 1980s (BBC News, 2006; Mbendi, 1998). Nigeria's debt grew largely due to penalties and late fees during the 1990s (BBC News, 2006). Nigeria has spent more than $41 billion to service her debt to Western creditors (Onuorah, 2001). In 2006, when Nigeria made a payment of $4.6 billion to the Paris Club, she became the first African nation to pay of its multibillion debts. Nigeria still will owe about $5 billion to other lenders, including the World Bank and the private sector (BBC News, 2006). The Paris Club canceled $18 billion of Nigeria's more than $30 billion external debt to it, but in return Nigeria had been forced to pay $12 billion on debt service (People's Daily Online, 2005). However, Hafez Ghanem, World Bank country representative in Nigeria, cautioned that, despite the debt exit of Nigeria from the London and Paris Clubs, the country's chance of sliding again into the league of debtor nations remains high if it depends on the external borrowings for funding her developmental projects. Considering Nigeria's poor performance, Ghanem urged that country to use her debt exit as a springboard "to take a quantum leap into development in this millennium through efficient utilisation of the freed resources in the post-relief period" (Nkwocha, 2007).

Owing to expanding revenues from oil in the 1970s, the country has endured sporadic economic growth (Lexis-Nexis, 2001). Starting with a limited number at independence in 1960, the country now boasts more than 2,000 industrial establishments (Embassy of Nigeria, 1998). However, successive governments neglect to invest in agriculture—the economic mainstay of the economy—prior to independence and the discovery of oil. About 70 percent of Nigeria's population is engaged in agriculture.

With the decline of oil revenues in the 1980s, Nigerians have endured about 20 years of economic stagnation under successive tyrannical military governments known for their corruption and ruthless hold on power (Lexis-Nexis, 2001). The nation's untapped oil reserve of 22 billion barrels is expected to be exhausted in 29 years (Akor, 2001).

Nigeria ranks as the 146th least developed of 174 countries analyzed by the United Nations Development Program's 1999 Human Development Report. The nation also has been classified, along with 34 other countries, in the low human development cadre because life expectancy, educational attainment, and adjusted real income are among the poorest in the world (Nwachukwu, 1999).

Eribo (2001) blames the African and Nigerian economic nemesis on the dogged, callous, and aggressive exploitation of the continent by Europeans. He contends that past and present African achievements hold promise for Nigeria and other African countries. He cites the victory of Nigerian Green Eagles in 1996 at the Olympic Gold Cup soccer. Cameroon won the contest in the 2000 Olympics. Eribo said Nigerians demonstrate their ingenuities in cities like Aba, Awka, Benin City, or Ibadan, where virtual illiterates dismantle, repair, and assemble foreign-made machinery and cars without reference to any manual.

Former head of state Chief Ernest Shonekan warned, "Nigeria cannot attain the democratic height and social stability she desires to without a vibrant economy capable of catering to her population" (Anyigor, 1998). To promote economic growth and social stabilty, Alhaji Maitama Sule, a former diplomat and Chairman of the Board of Trustees and Governing Council for the Shehu Shagari Institute for Leadership and Good Governance, called on the federal government "to fight corruption, encourage morality and good governance" (Anyigor, 1998). He called on the federal government to use traditional values to fight duplicity because Nigerian cultures condemned corruption.

With the return of a civilian administration in 1999, marking its Fourth Republic, the government introduced poverty alleviation programs to ensure that most Nigerians benefit from the economic revitalization. The Olusegun Obasanjo administration has taken steps to privatize and diversify the economy to ensure continued growth and encourage investment. The administration has turned a fiscal deficit into a surplus, but economic hardship remains prevalent (*Vanguard*, 2000, Aug. 28), while corruption, political, and religious crises continue to bedevil the country (*Vanguard*, 2006, Feb. 2006b).

National Profile of Nigeria

Table 2.1 paints a brief picture of Nigeria's socioeconomic context.

Table 2.1 Facts and Statistics on Nigeria

Official Name	The Federal Republic of Nigeria
Government	Three-tier structure: A Federal Government, 36 State Governments, and 774 Local Government Administrations
Official Language	English
Other Major Languages	Hausa, Fulani, Yoruba, and Igbo
Capital	Abuja (pop. 305, 900, est. 1992)
Major Commercial/ Industrial Cities	Lagos, Ibadan, Enugu, Port Harcourt, Benin, Jos, Calabar, Kaduna, Onitsha, Aba, Kano, Warri, Kano, Maidiguri, Enugu, Jos, and Nnewi
Currency	NAIRA; N1 . 00 = 100 k (one naira = hundred kobo)
Gross National Product (GNP)	US$29 billion (0.45% of US) in 1993; ranked third in Africa behind Algeria and Egypt
Real Gross Domestic Product per Capita	US$1540 (6% of US) in 1993; Nigerian ranks 21st in Africa, 17th in sub-Saharan Africa
Population	Estimates range from 120 to 130 million
Human Development Index (1)	0.400 (US = 0.940), ranked 137 (US = 20) of 174 countries
Status of Women	Gender-Related Development Index (2) = 0.380 (US = 0.923), ranked 108 (US = 4) of 137 countries. Women comprise approximately 36% of the wage-earning labor force.
Total External Debt	US$32 billion in 1993 (112th of GNP). Debt service costs were equal to another 29% of the value of goods and services exports (1992).
Major Subsistence Resources	Rice, maize (corn), taro, yam, cassava, sorghum, and millet
Major Commercial Resources	Sub-Saharan Africa's leading producer of oil, which accounted for 97.9% of total export earnings in 1992. Cash crops include cocoa, peanuts, palm oil, and rubber.
Main Ports	Lagos (Appa, Tin-can Island), Warri, Port Harcourt, One Deep Sea and Hub Port, Calabar (EPZ).
Main Industrial Complexes	Refineries and petrochemicals: Kaduna, Warri, Port Harcourt, and Eleme. Iron and Steel: Ajaokuta, Warri, Oshogbo, Katsina, and Jos. Fertilizer: One-Port Harcourt, Kaduna, Minna, and Kano. Liquefield Natural Gas: Bonny. Aluminum Smelter: Ikot Abasi and Port Harcourt.
Main Airports	Lagos, Kano, Port Harcourt, Abuja, Enugu, Kaduna, Maiduguri, Ilorinn, Jos, Owerri, Calabar, Yola, and Sokoto
Road Network	More than 15,000 km of intercity all-weather-paved roads, including dual carriage express trunks.

(continued)

Table 2.1 Facts and Statistics on Nigeria (continued)

Official Name	*The Federal Republic of Nigeria*
Railways	Two main lines (Southwest to Northeast; Southeast to Northwest) interlinked and terminatory at Lagos, Port Harcourt, Kaura, Namoda, Maiduguri, and Nguru. Major junctions at Kaduna, Kfanchan, and Zaaria. Gauge: 1,067 mm; Total length 3,505 route km.
Energy	Hydroelectric: Kainji, Jeeba, andShiroro. Thermal and Gas: Egbin (Lagos), Ughelli, Afam, Sapele, national grid for electricity distribution; national network (pipeline) for distribution of gas (under construction).
Education Profile	School is free and compulsory for students 6–11 years old up to junior secondary school. In 1991, 76 percent of children attended primary school and 23 percent attended secondary school. Adult literacy rate is 54 percent; male literacy rate is 64.7 percent; female literacy is 43.8 perecent (1993). A once distinguished university has deteriorated due to repression and underfunding.
Health Profile	Life expectancy 52.2 years for women and 49.0 years for men (1993). Infant mortality is 84 per 1,000 live births (1993), under age 5 mortality is 191 per 1,000 (1994), maternal mortality is 10 per 1,000 (1993), and 36 percent of children under the age of 5 are malnourished. There is 1 doctor per 5, 882 people (1988–1991). Public expenditure on health in 1990 was equivalent to 1.2 percent of GDP.
Religious Affiliations	Muslims 47.2 percent (mostly in the north and west). Christians 35.4 percent (predominantly in the south; 50% Catholic, 50% Protestant). Traditional religions 18 percent.
Area	356,669 miles [x2] (923,768 km [x2]), roughly twice the size of California.
Geographic Features	Nigeria is located in the West African region and lies between longitude 3 degrees and 14 degrees and latitudes 4 degrees and 14 degrees. It has a land mass of 923,768 sq km. About 35.6 percent of the land is arable, and 12.4 percent is wooded. It is bordered to the north by the Republics of Niger and Chad; it shares to the west with the Republic of Benin, while the Republic of Cameroun shares the eastern borders right down to the shores of the Atlantic Ocean, which forms the southern limits of Nigerian Territory. The 800 km of coastline confers on the country potentials of a maritime power. Land is in abundance in Nigeria for agricultural, industrial, and commercial activities.
	Situated in the tropics with an average temperature of 90°F (32°C). Annual rainfall varies from 98 inches (2.5 m) in the Southeast to 24 inches (0.6 m) in the North. Coastal forests cover the Southern regions, giving way to savanna in the North. The Niger River flows from the Northwest to join the Benue River in central Nigeria and then turns South form a fertile delta as it empties into the Gulf of Guinea.

Source. Africa Policy Information Center, 110 Maryland Avenue NE, #509, Washington, DC 20002.

3 Nigerian Advertising and Mass Media

MEDIA COMMUNICATIONS IN AFRICA

Like other societies worldwide, sophisticated forms of communication existed in Africa to exchange information despite diverse linguistic and ethnic differences among African peoples. Established forms of small- and large-group communication in African cultures include: an open market system, traditional ceremonies relating to agriculture and rites of passage, seasonal entertainment fairs, drums, town criers, storytellers, drawings, and physical communication (Ngwainmbi, 1995; Okigbo, 1989). However, modern mass media arrived in Africa along with the European scramble and partition of Africa in the mid-1800s. Print (newspapers and magazines) came first, then radio, motion pictures, TV, and now modern information and communication technologies (Hachten, 1993).

Beginning with the European introduction of the printing press, mass communication spread throughout Africa sporadically and unevenly as European colonial powers like Britain, France, and Spain developed and used them as a one-way system of communication from their seats of power to their territories worldwide. These mass communication outlets did not operate as forums for the mutual exchange of views and information on the colonies, but were used to promote colonialism and Western hegemony (Hachten, 1993; MacKay, 1964). Also, they were used to relay home news to the colonialists and white settlers.

Addressing the growth of modern mass media in Africa, Hachten (1993) stated that, like its sociopolitical and economic system, the mass media in Africa has experienced false "starts and reversals" as a result of decades of "economic stagnation—ineffective and wrongheaded centralizatized, socialist economies, government failures to support and encourage agriculture, misguided efforts at industrialization—as well as deeply embedded problems of poverty, illiteracy, ethnicity, and tradition, that broad catchall concept" (p. vii). These problems are coupled with political instability.

Of the almost 10,000 dailies in the world, Africa has about 200. In 1989, the continent had more than 105 million radio sets, although the number of TV sets remains quite small (Hachten, 1993).

NIGERIAN COMMUNICATIONS CONTEXT

The Print Media

Established in 1859 by the British Christian Missionary Minister the Rev. Henry Townsend at Abeokuta, the *Iwe Irohin Awon Ara Egba Ati Yoruba* was the first newspaper established in Nigeria and the first on the African continent published in an African language.

The history of the indigenous press started in 1863 with the establishment of Robert Campbell's *Anglo African in Lagos*. Published in English, this short-lived newspaper provided cheap and accessible information to educate and entertain its readers at a time when interest in Western education was on the rise. Although the British colonial administration founded some print outlets, nationalist newspapers grew in the late 1800s and early 1900s. During this period, indigenous press assumed the combative role of opposition to the autocratic colonial rule, fighting for independence. Although the number of Nigerian presses has grown since then, economic stagnation has hampered its growth in the last 15 years. Presently, the number of print outlets in Nigeria ranges from 150 to 180. The Nigeria press is known for its relative freedom.

Advertisements constitute between 28 and 35 percent of the newspaper content, with private newspapers carrying a higher percentage. Nigerian print advertising exists mainly in classified and display forms. Advertising in Nigerian magazines is not as extensive as newspaper advertising. The amount charged for various forms of print advertising is uncertain because most media outlets treat their prices as trade secrets and refuse to disclose what they charge.

Broadcasting

Radio broadcasting began in Nigeria in 1935 with the introduction of the British Broadcasting Corporation (BBC) Empire programs. Known as the Radio Distribution Services, the overseas services of the BBC dominated early radio broadcasting in Nigeria. To facilitate broadcasting nationwide as well as to encourage the introduction of indigenous programs, the Nigerian Broadcasting Service was established in 1951 and became a statutory body in 1957.

Chief Obafemi Awolowo, the premier of Western Nigeria, is credited with introducing the first TV station in Africa with the founding of TV service in Ibadan, the region's capital. Of Nigeria's 36 states, few own their own TV stations, but the subsidiaries of the Nigerian Television Authority (NTA) exist in most states. Nigeria has more than 40 AM and FM radio stations, 14 private TV stations, and 13 cable/satellite and cable retransmission operators. With the advent of modern information and communication technologies, Nigeria has been working to acquire additional information and communication technologies.

Like radio and print, it is unclear how much Nigerian radio stations charge for advertisements. However, advertising remains an important source of revenue for government-owned outlets and existing private stations. Advertisements are aired in blocks during and between programs. Nigerian TV also has commercialized news. Amienyi (1998) said that the government-owned network charges from $4,000 to $5,000 to cover events in the commercial capital of Lagos and other parts of the country.

Modern Information and Communication Technologies (ICTs)

With the growing role of ICTs in the global economy and their necessity for the economic development of emerging economies, the Nigerian government has set out some short- and medium-term objectives to develop an efficient and reliable telecommunications system (Aihe, 2006; Ndukwe, 2006). Like most emerging economies worldwide, Nigeria's telecommunications industries remains woefully underdeveloped. For example, there are more than 17 million people comprising 16,078,817 mobile lines and 1,207,707 fixed lines in a nation of about 130 million people. To leapfrog from her technological backwardness, since the return to democratic rule in 1999, the federal government has initiated policies and regulatory regimes aimed at modernizing and rapidly expanding the national telecommunications network and services in Nigeria (Aihe, 2006; Ndukwe, 2006). These measures call for deregulation, privatization, and foreign investments in Nigeria's telecommunication sector and has energized the telecommunication industry that remained moribund since independence.

Nigeria has launched the Nigerian Communication Satellite-1 (NIGCOMSAT-1), which is targeted for the application of telecommunications, broadcasting, Internet, real-time monitoring services, navigation, and global positioning systems (Deji-Folutile, Amaefule, & Ezeobi, 2007). China built and launched the satellite at a cost of $311 million after beating 21 other bidders in 2004 BBC, 2007). Critics allege that the huge amount spent on the grandiose project could have been better used to address the economic and social problems plaguing Nigeria (Raufu, 2003). However, government officials and supporters contend that the nation's satellites will enhance rural access to technology, the Internet, and boost Nigeria's and Africa's knowledge economy (BBC, 2007). It is estimated that the direct sale of transponders on NICOMSAT-1 would yield about $900 million between 2007 and 2022 (Deji-Folutile, Amaefule, & Ezeobi, 2007).

Cinema and Video

Introduced by the British during their colonial reign in Nigeria, films served as a vehicle to enhance the aims of colonialism and erode African heritages. Cinema outlets in Nigeria are concentrated in urban areas, but the number remains unknown. The medium appeals mainly to the young and well-to-do urban dwellers. Nigerian movie houses show mainly foreign movies from Europe, United States, China, and India. Advertising in movie theatres remains minimal.

In the past 15 years, the use of video has grown extensively. As the ownership of videocassette recorders grew, Nigerian-produced videos became an important source of entertainment because they were accessible and inexpensive. Video films produced in Nigeria have become popular in sub-Saharan Africa. Advertisers have not exploited this widely used and increasingly popular medium as a vehicle for marketing their products and services.

Strategic Communications

Newsom (2004) states that a variety of strategic communications, including financial public relations, integrated business communications, issues and crises management, lobbying and political communications, and government, exist in Nigeria. She observes that the incorporation of the Nigerian Institute of Public Relations in the country's law and the existence of strong undergraduate and graduate program in mass communication demonstrate the importance the country attaches to strategic communication as a vehicle for national development. She adds that that international public relations and international media relations are offered as special services available in Nigeria.

NIGERIAN ADVERTISING INDUSTRY

Modern advertising has existed in Nigeria for more than 150 years. About half a decade after the founding of Nigeria's oldest newspaper (*Iwe Irohin,* 1859), it began accepting fees to publish information.

The Nigerian Media Market Structure

Nigerian mass media outlets compete in two main markets: a consumer market for readership and listenership, and specialized markets for advertisers (Amienyi, 1998). The various forms of mass media (whether private or government owned) compete for the consumer market at the national level. However, Amienyi noted that the main competition among the mass media outlets occurs at the local level in the metropolitan cities of Lagos, Ibadan, Benin City, Enugu, Calabar, Aba, Port Harcourt, Jos, and Kaduna. The populations of these cities range from 400,000 to 6 million. The larger and more populated a city, the greater the number of media outlets existing in that city. For example, the commercial capital of Lagos remains the leading mass media market in Nigeria. Lagos, which has 15 newspapers, 10 radio stations, 8 TV stations, and a population of more than 6 million, remains the leading media market.

Amienyi (1998) said that the Nigeria market mirrors the situation in the United States, where a national circulating newspaper like *USA Today* is published in a metropolitan center, but distributes advertisements for businesses operating in that center and other parts of the country at local newsstands nationwide. A radio advertisement reaches people within a city, state, or region depending on number of miles its signals can travel. Most Nigerian radio stations are on the AM or FM dials. Although short-wave frequency is available, the Federal Radio Corporation of Nigeria (FRCN) dominates the frequency.

As the only outlets with a form of national network, government-owned NTA and FRCN could be described as the only sources of national broadcast advertising. This is because most state- and private-owned stations do not have networks and are incapable of covering the entire nation. It should be noted that local and international private-owned cable and satellite systems that reach the entire country have been on the rise since the 1990s. They have become a significant vehicle advertiser use to reach Nigerian consumers.

Advertising remains an important source of revenue for government-owned outlets and existing private broadcast stations. Advertisements are aired in blocks during and between programs and may include from 10 to 60 spots. The amount charged for these spots remains uncertain. The present study was unable to determine whether there is a limitation on the number of commercial breaks. Nigerian broadcasting outlets have commercialized news. Their charges range from $4,000 to $5,000 to cover events in the commercial capital of Lagos and other parts of the country.

Advertising Agencies

Nigeria has about 60 full-service advertising/public relations agencies. Most agencies in Nigeria are privately owned and are motivated by profits, but are expected to contribute to social mobilization (Okigbo, 1989). They are located in Lagos and other major cities. The number of indigenous-owned independent agencies has been growing in recent years. Some have begun to seek partnerships with foreign agencies in this era of globalization (Amuzuo, 2000b).

These agencies offer a full array of advertising and marketing services as well as research in the areas of market and opinion research and media analysis and evaluation. Advertising, public relations, and other forms of strategic communication, including political communication, exist at the strategic level in some companies, and the practice is offered as a specialty (Newsom, 2004).

Leading National Advertisers and Forms of Advertising

Studies have estimated the annual advertising expenditure in the Nigerian national economy to be N30 billion (at the time of this study, the current exchange rate of N90–110 to US$1). Of this number, the federal government accounts for a negligible amount of about (N10 million) (*Vanguard*, 2000, Feb. 21). The largest proportion of advertising and program sponsorships in Nigeria are provided by the subsidiaries of transnational corporations (Nestle, Unilever, Pepsi Cola, Coca Cola, and Toyota). Other advertisers and sponsors include indigenous manufacturers, distributors, banks, and breweries (Amienyi, 1998). In recent years, telecommunication providers have become great sources of advertising (Famoroti, 2005).

Obituaries, remembrance announcements, anniversaries, salutations, and other forms of congratulations and expressions dominate the majority of Nigerian advertisements. Product advertisements appear less frequently than personal types of advertisements such as obituaries and salutations. The most common advertised products are soaps, toothpaste, food condiments, laundry detergent, beverages, and nonprescription drugs.

As the medium of the masses, radio advertising remains significant. TV advertising in Nigeria is also important (Amienyi, 1998). The highest percentage of advertising monies is spent on TV. With regard to agency billings, Nigerian agencies are paid on a commission system instead of fees. The standard commission for placing an advertisement in a medium ranges from 15 to 20 percent (Ajayi, 2001).

Advertising Professional Organizations

Nigerian advertising professionals and businesses belong to Advertising Practitioners' Council of Nigeria (APCON), which monitors and regulates the activities of advertising agencies and practitioners in Nigeria (Amuzuo, 1999). It is a criminal offense to practice advertising without registering with APCON (Nwosu, 1990).

Many Nigerian practitioners belong to the Association of Advertising Practitioners of Nigeria (AAPN) (*ThisDay*, 1998) and the International Advertising Association (IAA). The IAA has about 40 Nigerian members who work to promote the value of advertising in Nigeria. These and other professional organizations in advertising, public relations, and journalism promote ethics and monitor the activities of advertising professionals and related professions.

Regulation of Advertising

Government agencies and professional groups regulate advertising in Nigeria (Amaechi, 1997; Amuzuo 2000a). Apart from APCON, several government agencies possess the authority to supervise and regulate Nigerian advertising. These include the Federal Environmental Protection Agency, which regulates outdoor advertising; the Central Bank of Nigeria, which deals with bank and financial advertisements; the National Insurance Commission, which regulates insurance advertising; and the National Agency for Food and Drug Administration and Control, which monitors food and drug advertising. With two or more government agencies controlling some aspect of advertising, practitioners continue to condemn and call for an end to multiple vetting of advertisements. They believe that if the process continues, it may "pose a colossal threat" to the development of the Nigerian advertising industry (Amuzuo, 2000a).

The vibrancy of Nigerian press and mass media extends to advertising. Nigerian advertisers are known to be creative. Creativity is not strictly regulated or restricted, but advertising messages are expected to be truthful. However, there is a tendency for Nigerian advertisers and creators to exaggerate claims. Weak rules, which are not enforced, enable advertisers to make exaggerated claims and violate existing advertising rules.

Most products, including cigarette and alcohol advertising, are placed in Nigerian mass media advertising, but cigarette and alcohol promotions are expected to carry a health warning.

Modern Technologies and Internet Advertising

Technology is driving the Nigerian advertising industry as it makes the transition from the manual to the computerized age. The industry is also making strong strides in regard to Internet advertising. Most indigenous advertising agencies rely on computer technology, and 50 percent of them are on the Internet (Amuzuo, 2000b). Internet advertising is growing, but can only be accessed by the rich because few Nigerian households possess home computers. Telecommunication companies are increasingly playing a significant role in the Nigerian advertising industry (Famoroti, 2005).

Nontraditional Media and Outdoor Advertising Media

Billboards are the primary form of nontraditional media used by advertisers. They dominate the landscape in Nigerian cities and have prompted the government to impose some degree of regulation. Other forms of outdoor advertising include posters and verbal hawking. Hawking takes place on streets and in passenger vehicles. Nontraditional media advertising such as trade directories, direct mail, transit, and air-blimps are almost nonexistent in Nigeria because such outlets are yet to evolve.

The Nigerian Consumer

With a population of more than 120 million, it remains difficult to find any systematic study that has examined the values and lifestyles of the Nigerian consumer. However, it has been noted that Nigerian advertisers tend to target the educated, the middle class, and the well to do. With regard to the masses, Nigerian advertisers tend to target those residing in the urban areas. Although Nigerian advertisers engage in "puffery" and globalization has led to increased use of Western appeals and advertising methods, Nigerian consumers are described as becoming increasingly aware and capable of sorting out advertising messages (Ajayi, 2001).

As a result of the economic recession of the past decade and a half, Nigerian consumers are resorting to cheaper goods, thereby leaving the manufacturing sector with heavy unsold stock, and thus producing an adverse effect on the economy (Ajayi, 2001).

Most Nigerian mass media outlets are based in the urban areas. Newspapers are barely circulated in rural areas. No concerted efforts have been made to reach those living in the rural areas, where more than 80 percent of the nation's population resides. Rural residents receive most of their information, including advertising, from the radio.

Cultural Values in Nigerian Advertisements

An analysis of the cultural and developmental messages and values in Nigerian mass media advertisements found that family and savings represent the most common developmental values used in Nigerian mass media advertisements (Alozie, 2005a). His study found that other positive and development-oriented values used in Nigerian mass media advertisements include service, gift giving, collectivism, wisdom, security and investment, proper health, honesty, love, and endurance. The analysis also found that some negative and Western-oriented values were used in Nigerian mass media advertisements. They include youth, conquest of nature, and image. The study also found that product features and benefits are the most popular traditional appeals found in mass media advertising.

Trends in Advertising and Marketing

Although conventional advertising dominates the Nigerian advertising industry, efforts are being made to move toward integrated marketing communication. Nigerian advertising practitioners believe that if the industry adopts integrated marketing, it will be able to diversify its offerings while enabling specialized agencies to evolve (Amuzuo, 2000b). For example, the industry has witnessed the emergence of independent media agencies and niche groups (*Vanguard*, 2000, Feb. 21). Indigenous agencies also hope to enter the global mass media arena by forming partnerships with foreign agencies. The industry is working to modernize by adding new technologies and Internet resources. The government has also embarked on deregulation that will allow the sector to grow and participate as the national economy improves (Amuzuo, 2000b; *Vanguard*, 2000, Feb. 14).

Direct marketing has become trendy in brand development, unlike the wholesale embrace of traditional advertising (Ajayi, 2001). Nigerian advertisements are accessing other countries, especially those in central and western regions of the continent. At the same time, globalization has led to an increased number of Western-produced advertisements found in Nigerian mass media (Ajayi, 2001). With the installation of democratic rule, various types of political advertising have also been growing as politicians and various groups use them to advance their goals (Newsom, 2004). She notes that politicians are employing consultants.

Advertorials

Advertorials as a form of strategic communication have a long history in Nigeria. They are used in politics whenever Nigeria returns political dispensation. During military administrations, groups use advertorials to bring to fore their concerns. However, they have been used dominantly by elites to promote their course.

4 Dynamics of International Relations, Culture, and Technology in the Era of Global Marketing

EVOLUTION OF THE DEBATE

Communications play an important role in human conduct and national and international affairs. However, the role of communications—especially international communications—has been besieged with controversies. The controversies deal with structural issues as well as the flow of information and its effects on national sovereignty (Allenye, 1995; Domatob, 1988; McPhail, 2006; Thussu, 2000; Uche, 1988, 1994, 1997). It should be noted that similar concerns exist within countries. For example, governments in developing countries are often accused of maintaining control of the mass media, thus influencing their contents to promote their policies and retain power (Domatob, 1988; Uche, 1988, 1994, 1997)

Since the turn of the 20th century, studies have established a link between communication and the evolution of international relations (Allenye, 1995; McPhail, 1987, 2006; Thussu, 2000). Allenye (1995) explained that most aspects of international relations, including those concerned with mass media, deal with power. He contends that there are two types of power related to communication in global affairs: the power of communication and the power of information. Although he observes that both concepts are related, he pointed out that a distinction exists between the two. He explained that structural issues such as ownership of mass media networks, technologies, and government policies give the founders of dominant world media systems the power of communication. However, he states that the ability to gather and influence mass media consumers to support an idea such as human rights, political freedom, and environmental protection are related to the power of information. The use of mass media artifacts enables the proprietors of the world media systems to achieve the later goal. It could be argued that the interlocked relationship between communication and information exists because one cannot do with the other.

To understand the role of communication in human conduct and international relations, it is important to define *power* and explain how communication and information are used to exert power. Allenye (1995) defines *power* as the "as the ability of to exercise control, to get others to do what they otherwise might not do were it not for your presence" (p. 4). Where power exists, the holder must find a way to get their subjects to do what they want the subjects to do. This is where the dynamic of power comes into play. According to Allenye, the consequence of power is often established when a person or group dominates one, but how the dynamic operates is subtle and remains a challenge to discern

Gramsci (1971) and Nye (1990) have addressed the dynamics of power in national and international relations. Depending on orientation, these scholars state that the sources of power include population, as well as territory, military, economic, political, cultural, and economic forces. These sources are also used to maintain power through forceful or nonforceful means. The dynamic application and operation of these sources to achieve, maintain, or impose power differ (Carr, 1939). Allenye (1995) agrees. He argues that those who play and set the conditions influence the rules, applications, and use of a particular dynamic. McPhail (2006) points out that Western countries dominate communicated-oriented supranational organizations like the International Telecommunication Union. Their domination enables them to set the rules governing international communication. These rules are constructed in favorable terms to the powerful nations at the expense of peripheral nations. For example, the international air waves are dominated by the core nations. Their text and software are the dominant source of information in most of the peripheral nations. An attempt by UNESCO in the 1970s to address these generated heated debate and fizzled as a result of strong opposition from core nations. Known as the New World Information and Communication Order, efforts to revive and attain the goals have not been successful (McPhail, 2006; Thussu, 2000).

The application international power could be structural or relational (Strange, 1988). *Relational power* refers to the ability to get an individual to do what he or she would not otherwise do without influence or coercion, whereas *structural power* is based on utilizing set rules and structure to direct and influence a person or society. Both of these concepts are involved in international communications. The former could be described as the use of Western-produced software (advertising, music, films, TV programs, and news) to influence people. The latter includes the dependence on Western-oriented technologies, policies, laws, and institutions to govern international communications.

This chapter relies on theories of globalization, imperialism, dependency, and convergence to analyze the role of international communication in global affairs, with an emphasis on political and cultural impact. Imperialism and dependency were included as analytical tools because of the ongoing debate that they become irrelevant to examine international affairs. Critics argue that globalization, convergence, and other theories related to the New World Order have overtaken them. The chapter also explores three specific strategic models in international advertising: standardized, adaptive, and country specific.

GLOBALIZATION

In 1964, when communication scholar Marshall McLuhan coined the term *Global Village*, he described it as the ability of the mass media to use technology to instantaneously relay information worldwide. He predicted that the Global Village would become a reality within the century.

Several factors have contributed to make his prediction a reality. These include advancements in telecommunications (Internet), technological equipment, the development of worldwide communication outlets, mass media conglomerates, and the growth of global corporations (Gershon, 1997; Hout, Porter, & Rudden, 1982; Levitt, 1983). Other factors include immigration, tourism, establishment of free trading blocks, and global marketing (Batra, Myers, & Aaker, 1996; Elinder, 1965; Mueller, 1996).

Jun (1994) pointed out that global businesses employ information and communication technologies to relay mass media advertising to reach consumers worldwide, increase the volume of their trade, and earn dividends on their campaigns. He identified the delivery of advertising messages as the primary means international business concerns use to persuade international consumers to purchase and use their products. The growth of global mass media, advertising, and public relations has prompted debates on the positive and negative impact of communication in the Third World (Allenye, 1995; Frith & Frith, 1990; McPhail, 2006; Thussu, 2000).

NATIONAL SOVEREIGNTY: IMPERIALISM, DEPENDENCY, AND CONVERGENCE

The Imperialism Context

Describing the structural theory of imperialism, Galtung (1971, 1980) contended that inequality within and between nations exists in every aspect of human activity. The desire to maintain dominance creates resistance to change. This resistance to change evolves from structural violence that permits a special type of dominance system. Galtung (1980) identified the four dimensions of achieving structural imperialism as exploitation, penetration, fragmentation, and marginalization. For example, Great Britain used the kingdom's technical, military, and economic superiority to dominate societies in Africa and Asia. Colonial rule enabled the British to penetrate, exploit, marginalize, and fragment the nations in these parts of the world.

Galtung (1971, 1980) described that dominance system as "imperialism." He pointed out that structural imperialism usually existed between collectives, especially among nations.

Galtung (1971) stated that imperialism is a concept that "splits up collectivities and relates some of the parts to each other in relations of harmony of interest and other parts in relations of disharmony of interest, or conflict of interest" (p. 81). Galtung contends that the theory of imperialism and the conflict of interest rear their bridgehead as a result of relationships in which the goals of the parties are incompatible. These goals represent the true interests of each party. They include sovereignty, living conditions, quality of life, cultural perversion, human or national subjects for self-preservation, and other demographic factors.

Given these struggles, nationalists, activists, and intellectuals have sought to define imperialism from a sociocultural, sociopolitical, or socioeconomic ground. Baumgart (1982) defined *imperialism* as "domination of one group over another group" to perpetuate the interests of the more powerful group. He said that imperialism could be spoken of in terms of cultural imperialism, religious imperialism, economic imperialism, and political imperialism. Azikiwe (1969) interpreted sociocultural imperialism to mean: "to command, to rule, to govern, to hold in trust, to civilize, to educate, to Christianize" (p. 50).

The Cuban revolutionist Ché Guevara viewed political imperialism as an unequal political and social relationship between classes and said that it must be subjected to radical transformation. Guevara contended that the concept is a contradictory historical phenomenon whose expansion creates conflict within a class, group, nation, or internationally (Petras, 1998). Economic imperialism may be defined as a system where the center (developed nations) has power over the periphery (developing nations) with regard to factors of production, such as capital, technology, communication, distribution, and manpower. The center nations use these factors to exploit and dominate the states in the periphery.

Building on Galtung's (1971, 1980) works, Anderson (1984) described communication and advertising imperialism as "the way in which advertising exchange between nations is structured internationally with the effect that some nations may dominate other nations and create a disharmony of interest between them" (p. 49). Elaborating on the relationship between center and periphery nations with regard to (international communication) advertising, Anderson (1984) said:

- The Center exercises domination by imposing a certain advertising structure on the periphery, and
- The Center penetrates the periphery by creating a center of local, internationalized elites to serve as bridgehead for the Center in its advertising spillover into economics, politics, culture, and other areas within the periphery society. (p. 50)

Uche's (1988, 1994, 1997) and Domatob's (1988) analyses of mass communication, cultural identity, and sovereignty supported these relationships with regard to Africa. Neocolonialism, Domatob stated, is an African reality that dominates every aspect of life, including the economic, social, political, religious, and cultural institutions.

The Dependency Context

The relationships between nations (center and periphery) have been explained through a related concept known as dependency. Critics of the unequal socioeconomic and cultural relationship between developed and developing nations claimed that mass communication and advertising promoted capitalism and perpetuated the cultural, economic, social, and political dependency of Third World countries on the West (Anderson, 1984; Cardoso, 1977; Roncagliolo & Janus, 1981Schiller, 1970, 1977; Sreberny-Mohammadi, 1997; Wells, 1972).

The dependency model is based on the notion that transnational corporations operating in the Third World take advantage of their technological, financial, managerial, operational, processing, and production superiority to impose their values and exploit the mineral and human resources in developing nations (Anderson, 1984; Wells, 1972). The dependency model charges that these transnational corporations collude with local interests and groups to deny upward mobility of the masses (Martins, 1982). This concept stipulates that Western institutions provide technological hardware, technical training, and capital assistance to develop the communication sector of developing nations. But the relationship remains one of exploitation and domination by the developed nations (Cardoso, 1977), instead of one of equality or one providing true assistance (Anderson, 1984; Schiller, 1970; Uche, 1988, 1994, 1997). Tansey and Hyman (1994) described the four tenets of the dependency model:

- Center-periphery: Relationship exists between advanced, developed countries and less developed countries because economic and political power is distributed asymmetrically between the center and the periphery.
- Many of the tenets of classical economics, especially the Theory of Comparative Advantage, do not apply to the economic development of the periphery.
- The Center realizes disproportionate gains from trade that favors it.
- Conspicuous consumption by the affluent minority impedes economic development in the periphery by diverting critically needed investment capital (Tansey & Hyman, 1994, p. 28).

Dependency theorists blame advertising and other forms of communication for undermining the cultural values of the developing nations

(MacBride, 1980; Roncagliolo, 1986). Roncagliolo charged that the Western domination of international communication and the business world promoted the welfare of transnationals and inculcated alien values without regard for the values and welfare of Third World residents. Explaining how transglobal advertisements from developed nations affect the culture of the peripheral countries, Freire (1993) said: "The invaders penetrate the cultural context of another group, in disrespect of the latter's potentialities; they impose their own view of the world upon those they invade and inhibit the creativity of the invaded by curbing their expression" (p. 133). Domatob (1988) argued that dependency is achieved through training, philosophy, economic orientation, and mass media programming. Uche (1994) contended that the demise of the communist bloc gave the West a free hand to capture and overwhelm the developing regions. He said:

> The collapse of communism has meant the collapse of a major alternative paradigm—the Marxist-Leninist model, that forced capitalism to develop a social welfare system for its marginalized productive labour force. This has led to a massive resurgence of neo-imperialism and the Western institutions that sustain it [such as the International Monetary Fund and the World Bank]. (Uche, 1994, p. 54)

Frith (1996) said that most advocates of the dependency model base their arguments on the impact of advertising that occurred more than 30 years ago, but the situation has changed. The success of emerging Asian economies demonstrated the need for reconsidering the dependency theory. However, Sauvant (1976) noted earlier that these countries did not follow their own paths in the economic development process. The recent financial crisis in Asia could be used to validate the argument of dependency modelists (Guttsman, 1997). These countries relied on Western financial sources and systems instead of finding local avenues to raise funds to sponsor their development programs. Reliance on Western sources left their economies vulnerable. When these economies went into recession and the cash flow from the West ceased, the economies collapsed.

Anderson (1984) said that transnational corporations produced goods for mass consumption. Mass production and rampant advertising, Janus (1980, 1981) contended, created artificial tastes, artificial consumption habits, and markets for unwanted and inferior goods. She argued that advertising helped transnational corporations to develop homogeneous consumption habits for goods (Janus & Roncagliolo, 1979). Janus (1986) blamed transnational corporations for dumping inferior goods and less nutritious food products at expensive costs in developing nations. She stated:

> The lifestyles promoted in advertising include implicit and explicit agendas for social relations, political action, and cultural change. In peripheral

contexts, where extreme economic inequality and political repression often create highly polarized societies, advertising helps to mask these profound contradictions with the message that the free enterprise system is the answer to society's problems. (Janus, 1986, p. 128)

A study by Martin, Chaffee, and Izcaray (1979) supported the claims that advertising created consumption and social alienation. Studying the role of advertising among the peasants in Venezuela, they found that the peasants became disenchanted after being exposed to products they could not afford (Lerner, 1963; Sinha, 1986). Kumar (1980) supports Janus' (1980, 1981) view that transnational corporations dump inferior goods in the developing world. He contended that transnational corporations manufactured goods in developing nations with the intention of marketing their products in their countries of origin. He said that transnational corporations produced better quality products for the consumers in their home countries, whereas those targeted toward and marketed in the developing host countries were outdated and of inferior quality.

Kumar (1980) said that products transnational corporations marketed in the developing world were unsuitable for their prevailing environments and did not meet their needs. The transnationals are able to behave as they do, Kumar said, because they "know for certain that if allowed to operate, they are likely to create effective demand for their product, whatever its utility" (p. 29) with the help of advertising. He said that transnational advertising hindered development, created dependency, and raised the level of social inequalities in developing nations because they operated with the goal of just making profits and supporting the status quo. There are numerous examples of this problem in recent years. Several American companies, including Nike, the producer of sports clothing, have been accused of exploiting their workers in some developing nations by underpaying them, not providing them with benefits, and allowing them to work under slavish conditions (Stewart, 1997).

Schiller (1970) argued that Third World mass media and advertising agencies did not receive adequate advertising revenue from local resources to support their operations. As a result, to exist, Third World mass media depended on the financial resources they derived from transnational advertising (Roncagliolo, 1986; Schiller, 1979). Roncagliolo and Janus (1981) said that the dependence of Latin American mass media on transnational advertising gave these corporations the power to control the local mass media. They pointed out that transnationals punished local mass media outlets that questioned their activities by withdrawing their advertising support. The control, they argued, enabled the transnational companies to perpetuate Western ideology and the values and policies of the elites in developing nations.

Tsao (1996) noted a Taiwanese case where the local agencies were forced to integrate at the request of their multinational clients because foreign-owned or joint ventures dominated the industry. These developments and dependencies, critics argued, weakened the independence of local mass media because they danced to the tune of multinational corporations to sustain their existence. Roncagliolo (1986) claimed the transnational power structure:

> Effectively intervenes in the national communications, through messages ensuring both its ideological presence and its basic economic function of articulating production and consumption by means of advertising campaigns. These campaigns are intended to widen markets in order to adapt them to levels of production achievable on the basis of the economic logic of maximization of profits. (p. 83)

As a consequence, critics of advertising claim that developing nations are unable to maintain an autonomous national communication system. Roncagliolo (1986) asserted that mass media in the developing nations were transformed into "advertising vehicles," which treated the public merely as a market offered to advertisers.

As stated earlier, detractors of advertising as a tool for national development underscore its negative impact on the economic growth of Third World societies. Mandell (1984) pointed out that advertising is want-creating. Those wants created by advertising, according to Lerner (1963), go unfilled in Third World societies because of inadequate disposable incomes. In light of this situation, critics might be correct when they claim that transnational corporations and their advertising activities create "alienation" and "dependent effects" and remain the "crucial mechanism" (Tantavichien, 1989, p. 8) for exporting and spreading Western values, consumption habits, and patterns of behavior (Hamelink, 1997; Martin, Chaffee & Izcaray, 1979; Sauvant, 1976). For example, U.S. tobacco companies have been accused of exporting and encouraging smoking in Asia and parts of the Third World as their market shares in the United States decline (*The Indian Express*, *The Financial Times*, & Reuters, 1997).

THE CONVERGENCE CONTEXT

Although the imperialistic and dependent nature of the relationship between Western transnational corporations and their host Third World countries continues to generate debate, Sarti (1981) describes the controversy as being somewhat simplified and contradictory. The imperialistic and dependency concept is challenged by proponents of convergence, who point to the advances in technology, telecommunication, and the rise and sustained growth of some Asian economies. They claim that these advances and successes undermine the arguments propagated by advocates of the dependency model. Convergence theorists contend that McLuhan's (1964) prediction of the world as a global village has been made possible by technology such as the Internet, satellites, and other forms of technical advances in communication that contributed to the growth of global trade and promoted cultural homogenization (Carey, 1989; Levitt, 1983). Remarking on the impact of technology in global trade, advertising, and communications, Levitt (1983), an advocate of global marketing, stated:

> A powerful force drives the world toward a converging commonality, and that force is technology. It has proletarianized communication, transport and travel. It has made isolated places and impoverished peoples eager for modernity's allurements. Almost everyone everywhere wants all the things they have heard about, seen, or experienced via the new technology. (pp. 92–102)

Frith (1996) described convergence as increased cooperation between nations, as well as the development of new and compatible forms of communication technology that were "creating a form of global integration that is unprecedented in the history of the world" (p. 8). She pointed out that the rise of the Four Dragons (South Korea, Taiwan, Hong Kong, and Singapore) as the world's most promising economies, and their continued growth since the 1980s, has dampened the dependency debate and renewed hopes about Asia's and other developing areas' economic development and modernization.

However, the economic and financial malaise that has plagued these countries in the second half of the 1990s, and their dependence on the financial assistance of the Western institutions and governments, compels the need to examine the relationship between activities of transnational corporations and their host countries in the Third World (Guttsman, 1997). Carey (1989) notes that the growth and globalization of communication has resulted in the "uprooting of people from meaningful communities" (p. 140), which has led to a decline in social, cultural, and political values.

Alternative Voices

Although the theories of imperialism and dependency continue to generate attention, some skeptics have challenged these concepts. For example, Sarti (1981) contended that the interpretation of these theories that form the basis for sociocultural and political debate appeared to be simplified. She argued that any consideration of the relationship (dependent or imperialistic) should not be generalized, but should be viewed in the specific historical context of each nation concerned. She emphasized the need for analysis in the role of communication and advertising for a particular region or country (Salinas & Paldan, 1979).

Sarti (1981) suggests there is a need for substantive studies to discern how communications influence the process of domination, who is affected, and how. For example, she states that the history of Latin America demonstrates that the impact of communication and advertising on national development differs from one country to another. This is due to conflicting results (both positive and negative) produced by studies that have analyzed the role of advertising on the national development of specific countries. Sarti said the differences might be explained by examining the impact of transnational communication in a specific historical context. Sarti's stance tends to agree with the notion that mass media and advertising can "contribute to the process of overcoming some problems of underdevelopment" (p. 317). Salinas and Paldan (1979) concurred with Sarti's perspective:

> There is a necessity for placing the analysis of the systems of communication within the frames provided by the specific sociohistorical formations that embrace them. In this respect, generalizations offered by a study centered upon the core of theinternational system most assuredly call for the complementary analysis of the particular forms in which is contained the dependent situation of the peripheral countries. (p. 86)

Some Latin American countries, such as Brazil, have shifted from simple dependency toward greater, but still asymmetrical interdependency (Straubhaar, 1991). Straubhaar (1991) said: "Audiences in many countries are also clearly expressing a preference both for national production and, particularly in the smaller countries, for intraregional exports, seeking great cultural proximity" (p. 55). Servaes (1991) identified some of the shortcomings associated with the dependency and imperialism debates:

- [Fails] to take into account the internal class and productive structures of the periphery that inhibit development of the productive forces[.]
- Tends to focus on the center and international capital as the cause of poverty and backwardness, instead of local class formations.
- Fails to differentiate capitalist from feudal (or other precapitalist) modes of controlling the direct producer and appropriating the surplus[.]
- Ignores the productivity of labor as the central point in economic development, and thus locates the driving force of capitalist development and underdevelopment in the transfer of the economic surplus from the periphery to the center[.]
- Encourages a Third World ideology that undermines the potential for international class solidarity by lumping together as "enemies" the elite and the masses in the center nations[.]
- [Remains] static, in that it is unable to explain and account for changes in underdeveloped economies over time. (pp. 59–60)

Bitterman (1985) argues that the common conceptions of a mass medium, such as advertising, as a villain that has undermined traditional values and promoted imperialism and dependency were unfounded. The debate "exaggerates the power of the vehicle as well as the arbitrariness and destructiveness of the influence, and it ignores the necessary complicity of culture in the process of change" (Bitterman, 1985, p. 38). She says, "transmission does not guarantee reception or influence. Where a culture does not understand or is not interested in the message—where no responsive chord is struck—the effort involved in sending it is wasted" (p. 39).

A study by Goonasekera (1995) supported that view. In a case study of four Asian countries (India, Japan, Malaysia, and Hong Kong), Goonasekera found that Asian viewers did not believe that Western programs corrupted their own. The Indians opposed banning foreign programs. They liked foreign news programs, but preferred locally produced, culture-specific entertainment programs. In Japan, the study found that foreign programs failed because domestic-produced programs were stronger and more qualitative. The Malaysians were favorably disposed toward foreign programs, but did not believe they enriched their culture. The Malaysians agreed that foreign programs exposed them to the outside world and increased their expectations of a better standard of living. They also said foreign programs were healthy for a nation with ethnic groups as diverse as theirs. However, they called for more local programming that reflected the cultural diversity of the country.

Global or Local Advertising: Which Model?

Since McLuhan's predictions in the 1960s that ICTs would lead in an interdependent global economy, other scholars have advocated the internationalization and standardization of marketing campaigns (Elinder, 1965; Fatt, 1967; Hout, Porter, & Rudden, 1982; Levitt, 1983). The practice and debate on international marketing, advertising, and public relations campaigns take three forms: standardization, adaptive, and country-specific campaign.

Known standardization, the campaign "refers to messages that are used internationally with virtually no change in theme, illustration, or copy—except, perhaps, for transmission where needed" for worldwide dissemination (Mueller, 1996, p. 139). Companies may adopt a campaign that has worked successfully in a domestic or regional market for a firm's global campaign and markets. Standardized advertising is created, developed, and implemented from the company's headquarters (Newsom, 2004). Advocates of globalization of marketing promotions state that falling trade barriers, world political stability, international investments, existence of international organizations, enhancement of technologies, emergence of trade blocs and agreements, and improved quality of goods have moved the world economy toward converging into common market, compelling businesses to adopt standardized promotional campaigns (Agres & Dubistky, 1996; Jain, 1993; Onkvisit & Shaw, 1987). Increased international travel, growing dependence on international trade, saturated domestic markets, improved economic conditions worldwide, higher profit margins in foreign markets, increased foreign competition in domestic markets, and population shift have been identified as factors that promote global marketing campaigns (Buzzell 1968; Frith & Mueller, 2003; Mueller, 1996; Prebble, 1992; Sorenson & Weichman, 1975).

Levitt (1983) renewed the debate and lent credence to advocates of standardized advertising when he contended that developments in ICTs have made the world smaller, thereby providing businesses with access to international consumers all over the world. He described the international consumer as an individual anywhere in the world who wants goods that are reliable, qualitative, and cheap. Advocates of standardized advertising claim consumers in Nigeria, Switzerland, Brazil, and Malaysia share common values, tastes and attitudes, and the desire to access high-quality products and services at competitive prices. They point out that standardized advertising helps corporations to save costs and compete.

Moriarity and Duncan (1990) enumerated several situational factors that influence the decision of an advertiser whether to standardize a campaign. These factors include product category, product life cycle, and strategic decisions such as objectives, targeting, positioning, branding, creative strategy, advertising theme and execution, media planning and buying, and research.

On the opposite continuum of the debate on standardization versus specialization are scholars who argue that distinguished cultural differences exist among people. Opponents of globalization argue that international campaigns should take into consideration these cultural differences. Called *specialized advertising*, this form of local promotion relies on customs, values, and norms to market a product in a particular region or country. Advocates of specialized advertising and marketing like Karruppur (1995) "recommend multi-domestic strategies on the premise that consumer heterogeneity continues to increase even within countries" (p. x).

Advocates of specialization offer three reasons that hamper the adoption of standardized campaigns: (a) lack of evidence for homogenization; (b) intracountry fragmentation; and (c) developments in factory automation, which allows flexible, lower costs and lower volumes of production and trade, are challenging the standard assumption of economies of scales (Segal-Horn & Davison, 1992). Lane, King, and Russell (2005) added the uniqueness of mass media as a fifth problem. They point out that few countries in the world provide the type of sophisticated media analyses found in the United States. They said that Americans are often frustrated by a lack of even simple circulation estimates for the primary media in foreign countries. In addition, they point out that agencies are often working with a complex set of guidelines from one country to another involving the amount of time or space devoted to advertising, the types of products that can be promoted, and the devastating execution of that are permitted.

Others argue that cultural socialization, political ideology and stability, religious beliefs, fear of domination, and socialization hamper standardization and contribute to the slow pace of adopting standardized campaigns (Al-Markty, Norman, Whitlow, & Boyd, 1996; Douglas & Dubois, 1977; Frith & Mueller, 2003; Garreau, 1981; Keillor et al., 1996). Opponents of standardized advertising press for specialized campaigns, although the basic principles of buying and marketing remain the same world over. They contend that successful cross-cultural marketing rests on using local values and appeals (Kotler, 1986; Zandpour et al., 1994).

However, a number of scholars, including some on the opposite end of the (standardized and localized) continuums believe that a compromise may be struck between the two—adaptive (James & Hill, 1991; Mueller, 1987, 1996; Newsom, 2004; Zandpour et al., 1994). They argue that standardized advertising may work for some products and in certain situations if advertisers produce advertisements that do not confront local sensibilities. These scholars believe such a compromise will enable advertisers to cut costs, project their image and product, and reach more international consumers. Also known as the third country-specific model, this form of campaign calls for the strategic planning, creation, production, and implementation of a campaign to be conducted with the boarders where the campaign will be conducted (Newsom, 2004). Country-specific campaigns are considered effective because consumers tend to prefer campaigns that reflect their values, rewarding advertisers who employ them (Boddewyn, Soehl, & Picard, 1986).

Studies have shown that multinational organizations rely on a mix of these models depending on global economic circumstance and prevailing political, cultural, infrastructural, and governmental policies existing in a country (Wells, 1994). Newsom (2004) pointed out that the periodic global economic downturns in the 1990s forced transnational public relations and advertising agencies to close their subsidiaries. The closure of these subsidiaries, she implied, became a blessing in disguise because it enabled the development and maturation of local agencies and promotional campaigns. Newsom also stated that the unsettled nature of the global economy affected societies and government policies. In some countries, the downturns led to liberalization of the economy and the mass media, whereas in other countries, it led to increased economic marginalization of the masses, thus spurring protests. Some governments reacted by increasing control over economic activity and the conduct of mass media.

The future of international promotional campaigns remains uncertain. The evolution of ICTs, trade agreements, immigration, and political changes will influence the process. Although the debate over standardization will continue to rage on, studies on the subject are likely to continue to produce contrasting results and viewpoints. However, businesses considering conducting promotional campaigns abroad should consider what worked in the past. For a standardized campaign to flourish, advertisers must ensure that their promotions do not clash with cultural beliefs. Rather, advertisements should be tailored to match different cultural orientations. If global advertisers take these factors into consideration, that effort may help them to achieve a compromise where their advertisements may employ some degree of standardization and localization (Douglas & Wind, 1987; Quelch & Hoff, 1986). According to Rijkens (1992), Unilever serves as a good example of a company that customizes its campaigns while maintaining "its name, its packaging, its basic consumer premise and the expression of this promise in terms of advertisements" (p. 96).

Advertisers must realize that, although the evolution of ICTs has made the worldwide transfer of information instantaneous, the world has not been transformed into a homogeneous society (Robertson, 1992). Cultural differences, varying degrees of technological and economic developments, and political and sociocultural differences hinder the comprehensive adoption of global advertising. The global consumer remains an elusive proposition, but could be reached if advertisers customized their promotion to reflect cultural differences. If international advertisers take into consideration the cultural differences that exist in the world, they would realize the need to find a middle ground with regard to promotional campaigns (Al-Markty et al., 1996; Frith & Mueller, 2003; Kanso, 1986; Mueller, 1996; Zandpour et al., 1994).

5 Advertising in the Information Age
Theoretical Perspectives on Culture and Technology

Children who grew up in rural Africa in the 1960s and 1970s recall with nostalgia those mornings when the town criers bang their gongs and sang to relay news to villagers. The beautiful sound of the gong and the town crier's sweet voice aroused children to start getting ready for school. As morning breaks, children meet up with siblings and friends at the square to attend school. This is especially true of those who have to walk some distance crossing rivers, bushes, and sacred forests to get to school. In sub-Saharan Africa, most villages have their sacred forests. They are usually thick, where children believe wild animals inhabit and ghosts and native gods reside. Most children must have heard frightful folklores about sacred forests, making them afraid to cross those areas alone. Even if you are in the company of others, getting to these areas produces goose bumps and hair-raising experiences. The echoes of birds and other animals add to your feelings, cultural orientations, and spiritual development and knowledge. These experiences form their relationships with nature, community, family, teachers, spirits, God, gods, and authority figures. These values and experiences influence their choice of doing good or bad, serving your community, and respecting the natural order. The forests serve as sources of stable food (Alozie, 2005b).

African children of today are not benefiting from these formative experiences because traditional cultures, values, and ecology are disappearing. Societies worldwide are being bombarded with messages, values, symbols, and philosophical orientations of the West. Advertising serves as a primary conduit for conveying these messages. Nowadays, rural African children are not likely to wake to the sounds of gong and the voice of the town crier, but rather to broadcast signals or the blaring horn of a vehicle cruising on the scared forests their parents walked by. They may not have heard of the folklores surrounding their sacred forests, but have grown accustomed to watching Western soap operas. They may not have learned that their fathers once hunted the bush surrounding the sacred forests to catch an animal for meat, and their mothers farmed for cash and food crops. Sacred forests are usually untouched. In the guise of development and globalization, most African sacred forests and vegetative lands have been destroyed. The wild animal, native crops, and commodities are becoming extinct. The sacred forests have been or are being destroyed to build highways, build industrial parks, extract minerals, and establish industrial agriculture. Mega cities are encroaching into hitherto untouched land (Alozie, 2005b).

In *Conserving Culture*, Redner (2004) blames the disappearance of traditional cultures and the loss of biological diversity and the environment on globalization thatICTs are propelling and exacting. With Western free-market philosophies and values holding in emerging countries, Redner contends that the world's diverse cultures are growing increasingly homogeneous, thus evolving into a monoculture. Global culture relates to the growing indistinguishable tastes, activities, aspirations, lifestyle, values, and other human manifestations globally. Redner argues that global culture has produced an overwhelming effect: the extinction of a variety of traditional values and biodiversity.

Studies on culture, advertising, ICTs, and globalization are common with regard to developed nations and some developing nations in Asia, but few dealt with Africa with regard to their impact on most Africa societies as this text does. Thus, this chapter uses technological and cultural theories as its conceptual framework to explore the connection between advertising and ICTs. It is important to discuss how ICTs have ushered in an era of global economic, political, and cultural interconnection and dependence. The impact of these developments remains a subject of intense debate considering their connection with advertising.

THEORY OF TECHNOLOGY

Technological Determinism

As the Information Age dawns, which Marshall McLuhan predicted during the first half of twentieth century, the debate about the role of technology in human development is center stage. The Information Age is described as a period when dependence on information will become the mainstay of the world economy (Whetmore, 1995). It marks a period based on service instead of manufacturing, when a majority of the labor force will be employed to produce, manufacture, and retrieve information and data with computers. It is suggested that acquiring and employing ICTs has the potential to assist developing nations to transform their economies from backwardness into modern states.

In a nutshell, technological advocates claim that ICTs promise a "utopian" society, where the lack of food, water, shelter, clothing, and access to information will cease to exist, and plagues such as famine, drought, infant mortality, epidemics, and war can be overcome. These transformations and promises will be fulfilled because ICTs will enable developing nations to operate a knowledge-based economy.

This prediction and promise are not new. Third World leaders and development planners have been aware of these potential breakthroughs for more than 50 years. Western scholars have advocated the view that ICTs remain the vehicles that will enable developing nations to sail out of their economic abyss into economic prosperity (Lerner, 1963). This dogma has been described as "social construction." Social constructionists contend that human and societal needs dictate the course of technological innovations, and, further, that technological changes could be directed and used to benefit humanity and developing societies.

This view is contradicted by "technological determinism" (Hughes, 2000). Technological determinists view technology and technological innovations as independent forces outside human control. Moreover, they claim that technological innovations dictate and influence the course of human and societal developments. Hughes (2000) offers a third concept—"technological momentum." Technological momentum is based on the notion that "newer, developing systems {technologies} are generally more open to societal influences than more mature developing systems, which are more resistant to external influences and thus more deterministic" (p. 26).

African experiences with technologies as vehicles for social modernization and economic development remain unclear and uncharted. ICTs have been used as a conduit to relay advertising to African and other Third World countries. Thus, advertising has become a vehicle of exposing traditional societies to Western values, thus influencing their values. As Roberts (1987) and other scholar points out, the exposure has undermined the cultural values in these societies (Alozie, 2005b; Anderson, 1984; MacBride, 1980; Schudson, 1984).

CULTURAL THEORIES

As a form of social communication, advertising tends to reflect the values of a society (Cheng, 1997). As a cultural communication, advertising is capable of redefining and influencing individual and societal values. Differences that exist within, between, and among cultures influenced Hofstede's (1980) definition of culture. He defines *culture* as "the collective programming of the mind which distinguishes the members of one human group from another" (p. 25). He explains that values create "a broad tendency to prefer certain states of affairs over others" (p. 19). Values tend to regulate members of society by identifying right from wrong, success from failure, and acceptable from unacceptable behavior. Samovar and Porter (1994) describe cultural values as "a set of organized rules for making choices, reducing uncertainty, and reducing conflicts within a given society" (p. 15).

Scholars have developed world cultural theories and value systems to explain the differences in cultural values that exist worldwide, including: Hofstede's Four Dimensions of Culture, African Value System by Obeng-Quaidoo (1986) and Moemeka (1997), and Murdock's (1955) Common Denominator of

Cultures (Universals). Others include Hall's (1959) Primary Message System and Hall and Hall's (1990) High-Context versus Low-Context Cultures.

African Core Value System

African Value System by Obeng-Quaidoo (1986) and Moemeka (1997) identifies core Africa values as (a) religion as a way of life, (b) supremacy of community and value of the individual, (c) sanctity of authority, (d) the concept of work and relationship to nature, (e) value of time and its influence, and (f) respect for old age.

Religion as a Way of Life

Traditional African religions (excluding Islam and Christianity) recognize two types of gods: the Supreme God, who is believed to be far away and unreachable in the physical world, and lesser gods, who serve as intermediaries to the Supreme God. Religion is present and persuasive in the routine of African life. Africans consult their gods through native doctors to determine the outcome of major events in their lives, such as marriage, examinations, job promotion, farm production, money matters, travel, and even murder.

Supremacy of Community and Value of the Individual

African cultures recognize the value of the community over the individual. In African communalistic cultures, the welfare of the community supersedes the interests of the individual. Individuals must sacrifice their welfare for the welfare of the community. Emphasis placed on the community's welfare does not negate the values and rights of the individual. Therefore, the welfare of the individual is viewed as an extension of the community.

Respect for Old Age

Africans celebrate old age. The elderly are regarded with dignity and respect. Those who attain old age are viewed as having honored their duties, obeyed the Supreme God and the lesser gods, adhered to cultural mores, and worked for the good of the community. The elderly men of the community are viewed as the repository of knowledge and wisdom because of their experiences and longevity. The old have more wisdom than the young. Therefore, the young should respect as well as learn from them. Knowledge is transferred through oral tradition.

The Sanctity of Authority (Leadership)

In traditional African societies, leadership comes from three sources: appointments, elders in a community, and parents. African cultures view formal leadership roles as positions of honor, service, and responsibility. Appointed leaders earn their positions as a result of a record of good conduct, fairness, and generous contributions to the welfare of a community. Another source of leadership and power in Africa is age, sometimes called *gerontocracy*. Gerontocracy is an informal leadership by age and wisdom involving every member of the society except the very young.

The Concept of Work and Relationship to Nature

Africans view industrial work as a means of earning subsistence living for survival. They do not regard industrial work as an eternal way of life or a duty as Westerners do. When Africans lose their industrial work, they do not react negatively to job loss as Westerners do because they do not believe wealth can be obtained from industrial work. Farming and nature are viewed as sources of wealth.

The Value of Time and Its Influence

African value systems do not view time in the linear fashion as Western cultures do. In most African cultures, time does not possess an indefinite past, present, and finite future. Among Africans, the concept of time is thought of as symbols of events. Time is viewed as a composition of events that have occurred: those taking place now (immediately) and those that may occur in the future. Obeng-Quaidoo (1986) said that the future is absent in the African concept of time because time and events that are expected to happen in the future do not constitute time because they have not happened. This means that Africans view time as a two-dimensional phenomenon—a long past, a present, and no future.

Hofstede's Four (1980, 1983) Dimensions of Culture

Hofstede conducted a study in which he surveyed people from more than 50 countries to establish national differences in work-related value patterns of various cultures. To do so, he administered 32 value questions to employees of subsidiaries of the same multinational corporations in different countries and in various regions of the world. From the survey, Hofstede derived four values: power distance, masculinity/femininity, individualism/collectivism, and uncertainty avoidance.

Power Distance

A common adage in most societies states that all fingers are not equal. This adage contends that the distribution of power, wealth, and level of intelligence remains unequal in most cultures. In his study, Hofstede describes power distance as the extent to which a society accepts the concept that power in their institutions and organizations is distributed unequally. These institutions include families, corporations, schools, and communities.

In societies like Japan, Mexico, and the Arab world, strict and vertical structures exist and are emphasized. Subordinates depend on superiors to provide directions and do not act on their own initiative. They wait for instructions from the top. In contrast, in countries like the United States, Great Britain, and Sweden, a greater degree of equality and informality exists. Subordinates initiate actions and do not have to defer to their superiors for every action taken. Inequality of power also exists among nations. Compared to most Western cultures, Nigerian culture fosters greater high-power distance. Nigerian culture recognizes inequality by age, socioeconomic status, and knowledge. Nigerian culture considers it rude when a young person addresses an elder person by their first name. Nigerians believe that wisdom is gained through age (Olaniran & Roach, 1994).

Individualism-Collectivism

These terms describe the extent to which a society places value on the welfare of an individual over that of a group. In individualistic societies, the primary concern of a person deals with his or her welfare and that of the person's immediate family. In collective cultures, individuals—through birth and possibly later events—belong to one or more close "in-groups" (families, clans, communities, and organizations) from which they cannot become independent. The in-group protects the interests of its members in exchange for loyalty. Collective societies are tightly integrated, whereas individualistic societies are loosely integrated. Hofstede notes that individualistic tendencies are grounded in developed and wealthy nations in Europe and the United States, whereas collectivistic tendencies are established in less developed parts of the world. Considering the emphasis placed on extended family and friendships, Nigerian culture exhibits more collectivistic properties than most Western cultures (Olaniran & Roach, 1994).

Masculinity/Femininity

These characteristics are used to establish the social roles of men and women. In masculine societies, men are expected to be assertive, ambitious, and competitive. They are also expected to strive for material success and demand respect. These societies include Japan, Italy, Jamaica, and West Germany. Women are expected to provide nonmaterial services to improve the quality of life. Children are viewed as being weak and must be protected. Conflicts are resolved by force.

In feminine societies like Finland, Portugal, Thailand, and Chile, the role of men and women overlap. Neither gender is expected to be competitive or ambitious. In these societies, success and wealth are not highly regarded; rather, greater value is placed on friendship, spirituality, and dignity. They pursue different qualities of life and offer room for those in society who are weak and slow to develop their potential. However, in both feminine and masculine societies, the political and work values, as well as institutions, are usually male-dominated. Olaniran and Roach (1994) said that Nigerian culture exhibits both masculine and feminist characteristics, but remains less masculinistic. Nigerian feminist tendencies are demonstrated through its feministic nurturance and the prominence placed on extended family and friendships. However, Olaniran and Roach said that Nigerian culture is growing increasingly masculine because of the erosion from nurturance toward self-sufficiency, material acquisition, and greater sex role differences.

Uncertainty Avoidance

This explains the extent to which people feel threatened by ambiguous situations. As a result, they depend on established beliefs and institutions to help them avoid the situations they consider to be unstructured, unclear, or unpredictable. Depending on the culture, the structures that are used to avoid uncertain situations include religion, technology, and legislation. Countries with strong uncertainty-avoidance values include India, Denmark, and the Philippines. These cultures believe that uncertain events are dangerous. They are active, aggressive, security-seeking, and intolerant. Peru, Greece, Portugal, and France are cultures that possess weak uncertainty-avoidance values. Cultures with weak uncertainty-avoidance inclinations are contemplative, less aggressive, unemotional, accepting of personal risks, and more tolerant.

With regard to communication, Nigerian culture accepts greater ambiguity in communication contexts. In some communication contexts, the Nigerian communication process often requires interlocutors to fill in unspoken words or agree with the information (Olaniran & Roach, 1994). When considering information obtained from mass media, Nigerians tend to depend on more than one news source to put any information in context.

Universal Cultural Theory

Murdock's (1955) Common Denominator of Cultures (Universals) concerns the modes of conduct and behaviors common to all cultures. Universals include biological needs such as a sense of hunger and eating to ensure survival. They also refer to human needs such as the transmission of knowledge from one generation to another. For example, Hinduism recognizes a universal dharma that includes truth telling, avoiding unnecessary injury to others, and faithfulness. Culturalists believe the manners by which these drives and needs are responded to and met are shaped or determined by cultures.

Murdock (1955) identifies common values among societies in the world as: age, age grade, athletic sports, bodily adornments, calendars, cooking, courtship, education, etiquette, family, folklore, funeral rites, gestures, gift giving, incest taboos, joking, kin groups, tool-making, magic, marriage, mealtimes, mourning, mythology, property rights, religious rituals, and weather control, to mention a few common values among societies in the world.

6 The Digital Divide and Status of Sub-Saharan Africa

Marketing in an Interdependent Global Economy

The dynamics of international relations and marketing have been evolving over the past two decades. Shrinking population in developed nations, increasing population in the developing countries, fall of communism, and development of ICTs and globalization contributed to the evolution in international business. A product or service developed in Japan, the United States, or Germany cannot be sustainable, viable, or profitable if consumers in Brazil, China, and South Africa do not demand it. To bring attention to their products and services and gain domestic and worldwide acceptance, manufacturers are increasingly relying on advertising as a key marketing medium in this era of globalization. ICTs serve as major conduits for transmitting advertising and other media artifact to consumers worldwide.

Globalization of the world's economy offers both promises and challenges. The promises concern the ability to navigate, reach, and gain access to consumers worldwide, thus improving the profitability of businesses. However, access to the worldwide market and consumers comes with challenges. These challenges include navigating the political, economic, social, cultural, and legal environments, as well as the availability of infrastructures in a world where differences in economic development, technological status, and values exist. In view of this debate, this chapter, while exploring the role of ICTs in socioeconomic development, establishes what is missing in the debate dealing with the impact of globalization and the digital divide in countries in sub-Saharan Africa. It reexamines the social, economic, and cultural conditions of these countries under which the current changes and movement toward a global and technological world will take place. It also examines some of the issues dealing with the transfer, content, development, and management of information and media technologies, as well as assesses the reasons that the digital divide persists and, in conclusion, offers some area-specific solutions.

This exploration employs political economy to examine the process of acquisition, consolidation, diversification, commercialization, internationalization, the work of the profit motive, as well as the relationship among ICTs, advertising, and societal development (Boyd-Barrett, 1995). Political economy deals with the exploration of structures of economic and political power of theorizing communication (Thussu, 2000). To address these subjects, this chapter is guided by the following questions: (a) What are the major challenges in infrastructure, human resource development, application, and content in sub-Saharan Africa? (b) What course of action is being taken to close the gulf? (c) Should governments in sub-Saharan Africa focus on and invest heavily in ICTs in the face of existing harsh socioeconomic conditions and inadequate provisions for information and communication infrastructures? (d) How will technology affect advertising in Nigeria and other nations in sub-Saharan Africa in this era of globalization?

POLITICAL ECONOMY AS A CRITICAL APPROACH

Scholars are increasingly applying the interpretative vehicle such as political economy to a wide range of subjects, including consumer behavior, culture, government policies, economic, and social issues. Qualitative approaches represent a paradigm shift from the positivist "hard science" perspective, which has traditionally dominated modern science and academic studies.

The positivist belief advocates the cardinal tenets of universal truth, objectivity, reality, knowledge independent of its context, and separation of researcher from the research subject. In contrast, the move to interpretivist mechanism, also referred to as "postpositivism" or "postmodernism" (Firat & Venkatesh, 1995), explores the opposing viewpoint, such as socially constructed truth, subjective reality, knowledge that is context-dependent, and the presence of the researcher in the phenomenon being studied (Hudson & Ozanne, 1988).

Political orientation influences the course of development in most societies. Inayatullah (1967, 1976) explained that a society's political perspective possesses significant implications for development because it determines how a society accomplishes increased control over environment, increased control over its own economic destiny and government, and enables individuals to increase control over themselves. History, cultural, and moral values create the need for societies everywhere to be able to control her destiny and determine the course of societal and human development.

Political economy, which originated in Great Britain, deals with the study of the economic process. While assuming power is unevenly distributed, it explores the relationship between micro- and macroforces in economic development. The school also investigated how a government's practical political actions and policies on finance and commerce interact with the pure economic realities of production, finance, and trade. Adams Smith, David Ricardo, Jeremy Bentham, and Thomas Malthus are regarded as classical economists who championed the study of political economy.

Classical political economists were mainly concerned with growth and development. They were interested in studying the nature and causes of the wealth of nations and the distribution of the national product among the factors of productions: land, labor, and capital. They assumed the economic challenge of any society as the struggle to produce wealth from nature in view of the growing population and finite resources of nature and private-market forces. To harness the wealth of nature, classical political economists believe the focus of an efficient economy should be concerned with the exploitation of labor. Labor, they argued, confers values on goods. They argued that capital accumulation, expansion of market, and division of labor influence economic behavior, but these factors are governed by natural law and self-interest.

Classical economists did not endorse laissez-faire dogmatically. They advocated government intervention to ameliorate and correct the failures and harsh outcomes of the competitive market economy. They called for utilitarianism because the approach emphasized communal welfare. Rather than being upholders of natural rights, they called for government action when public good demands it (Mosco, 1995).

A second school of thought has emerged from this school. Known as neoclassical economics, this school of thought is concerned with the most efficient allocation of scarce resources among competing interests, whereas classical economists are more interested in expanding resources and allocating them to stimulate growth. Neoclassical economists believe that supply and demand (and their underlying cost and demand condition) influence prices, whereas classical economists believe that prices are derived from natural rates of reward of factors of production.

Application

Comeliau (1995) pointed out that development emanates from a society's political process, rather than from ordinary technocratic know-how. This relationship, he explained, compels choices between different goals and arbitration, between interest groups, and, hence, a constant interplay of power relationship, ideological confrontation, and negotiating strategies. This accounts for the use of political economy to examine how internal and external factors influence policies of socioeconomic development. Mosco (1995) offered five distinctive characteristics of political economy as analytical tools:

1. Social change and historical transformation—the implications of ongoing evolution are examined within longer time frameworks;
2. "Totality of social relations—considering specific interrelationship between politics, culture, economics, and ideology;
3. Commitment to moral philosophy—providing a critical elaboration of the principles and values that create and influence behavior to ensure that a balance among values of self-interest, materialism, individual freedom, human labor, and democracy; and
4. Social praxis—the unity of deliberation and acting are explored.

Boyd-Barrett (2002) refers to Mosco (1995), who points out that when the political economy discusses media, it is concerned with procedural and structural aspects:

1. Process of commodification: Deals with the process and transformation of measuring market value in terms of use and to measure values in terms of exchange in the market place.
2. Process of spatialization: Explores the mechanism of prevailing over the constraints of space and time in social life.
3. Process of structuralization: Examines the Marxist maxim and dialectic that explores under what conditions people who make history are produced.

Based on these contentions, an analysis based on political economy requires addressing the following areas:

1. Analysis of media in historical, social, and political terms;
2. Addresses media relations to politics, economics, and ideology;
3. Has a moral purpose; and
4. Its endpoint is social action context. (Boyd-Barrett, 2002, p. 49)

Mosco (1995) identified five conceptual steps for conducting research and understanding political economy:

1. Realist: Accepting discourse and social practices as authentic;
2. Inclusivity: Explains the present by honoring the trends and modes of the past;
3. Moral: Indicates its interest in moral issues and outcome.
4. Constitutive: Epistemology that rejects economic forces as an adequate basis for understanding.

Critical concerns in political economy deal with its analytical nature, which exposes shortcomings in orientations, while striving to improve the system as it seeks to calm tensions between standings on certain issues (Boyd-Barrett, 2002).

DOMINATION OF CORE NATIONS

When more than 79 percent of the world's 5.7 billion people are engaged in the struggle for food, water, shelter, clothing, and access to information, whereas just under 20 percent control the world's resources, coasting in abundance and lusting in consumerism—a struggle rages—a Third World War—of sorts. This war is being waged between the wealthy nations of the North and the poor nations of the South. It may not be as hot as World War I or II, which the globe experienced in the first half of the twentieth century, nor as suspenseful as the Cold War, the ideological struggle that the West and East endured during the second half of the last century, but the economic and sociocultural impacts are as grave as the hot and cold wars.

In an era when technological breakthroughs have made the world smaller and have created greater prosperity in Northern societies, the current war remains economic, political, technological, and sociocultural. It is euphemistically referred to as the "divide(s)." The divide(s) is as brutal as a hot war and as mischievous as the Cold War. Because the North is not bearing the brunt of the suffering, it attracts scant media attention. The suffering is borne mostly by Southerners in Africa, Asia, and Latin America.

In recent years, of all the divides, the gulf in ICTs, known as the "digital divide," has attracted the greatest attention. This could be attributed to the view that, historically, technological superiority has always served as the mechanism for domination and exploitation. Past and current technological gulfs have been blamed for creating and perpetuating economic and sociocultural divides and imperialism (Mendelssohn, 1976; Ziegler & Asante, 1992). Although new ICTs are transforming the way Northern societies interact, conduct business, compete in the international market, deal with social welfare issues, and set the agenda for national development (Sussman, 1997), Southern societies, especially countries in sub-Saharan Africa, are being left behind (Mutizwa, 2000). In addition to poverty, disease, famine, corruption, and war, they are plagued with both lack of access to information and the capital necessary to build the infrastructures needed to join the Information Age.

As ICTs force the world to become increasingly interdependent, it is also creating a wider economic gap between the North and South. These technologies are being used to convey Western software, such as advertising music, news, and TV programs, into Africa without reciprocal exchange. This imbalance, coupled with the hegemony of global capitalism, has compelled activists to voice their opposition (CNN.com, 2001). During the 1990s, there were peaceful as well as violent protests in the major cities of Asia, South America, Africa, North America, and Europe to protest globalization, capitalism, and rapid technological advances.

In January 2001, two meetings—one in Davos, Switzerland, and the other in Porto Alegre, Brazil—took place to influence the course of this struggle for human dignity. The World Economic Forum in Davos, which has taken place annually for several years, received most of the media attention. Predominantly attended by Northern corporate and national leaders with a token Southern presence, the Davos Forum advocates globalization and technological advances as the mechanisms for promoting global exchange of economic, technological, and sociocultural activities and transformation.

In contrast, the World Social Forum, billed as an anti-Davos Forum, was held for the first time. Dominantly attended by Northern activists, with a token presence by their Southern counterparts, the attendees opposed globalization and advocated the need to ameliorate the impact of technological advances on Southern nations, such as those in sub- Saharan Africa. At the meeting's conclusion, the Davos Forum called for continued efforts to integrate the Southern nations into the global economic and information exchange to help them reap the fruits of technological promises, whereas the Porto Alegre

Forum advocated caution, if not abandonment, of the current rush to adopt globalization and technological advances as the mechanism to improve the lot of the masses in developing nations.

SOCIOECONOMIC CONDITION OF SUB-SAHARAN AFRICA

Taking a philosophical view toward describing the West's craven exploitation of Africa's wealth, which has contributed to the popular perception of most of the continent as a place of suffering; a place of wars; a place of oppression; a place of hunger, disease, ignorance, and backwardness; and a debt-ridden region, Mozambique's President Joaquim Chissano said:

> The owner needs the cow because of its milk. The cow needs the owner because he provides it with hay. But when the cow ceases to produce milk, the owner may well decide to slaughter it. The cow cannot do the same to the owner. (*Electronic Mail and Guardian*, 1998, Nov. 4).

Chissano's allegory relates to the socioeconomic predicaments of the 53 African nations subjected to centuries of European marginalization of Africa through slavery, colonialism, exploitation of her natural resources, neglect of the continent's social institutions, and imposition of Western economic values and debt.

In the 1999 rankings of the Human Development Report (HDR), the United Nations Development Program (UNDP) classified more than 30 African nations into the low human development category out of the 174 countries in the ranking. Sierra-Leone was at the bottom of the list in the lowest category (Nwachukwu, 1999). Based on gross national product (GNP) per capita, the world's economies are classified into three groupings: low-income ($610 or less in 1990), middle income ($611–7,619), and high income ($7,620 or more) (Mueller, 1996). With a population of more than 700 million, Africa's GNP combined was less than $150 billion (Ihonvbere, 1997b).

Referring to Chissano's statement, the *Electronic Mail and Guardian* (Nov. 4, 1998). states that "the cows are the 41 poorest countries of the South, still linked umbilically to their owners, the wealthy countries of the North, to which they owed $215 billion at the end of 1997." Ihonvbere (1997b) and the *Electronic Mail and Guardian* (May 18, Nov. 4, 1998) point out that as the 1990s ended, the debt was expected to top $300 billion, of which Africa would be accountable for $222 billion (about R1 356 billion in South African currency). Describing nations in sub-Saharan Africa as cows that have ceased to produce milk, *Electronic Mail and Guardian* (Nov. 4, 1998) contends that the world's poorest nations cannot pay their debts and provide the basics (food, shelter, education, and health care) to their masses.

Explaining the socioeconomic situation of sub-Saharan Africa during an address at the 1994 conference of the International Press Institute in Cape Town, South Africa, an official of UNESCO said:

Most African countries emerged from the struggle for political independence only to find themselves engaged in struggle for food, water, shelter and clothing in the face of ever-increasing population growth rate, of low life expectancy, high infant mortality, and continuous political and economic strife, resulting in millions of refugees. (Yushikiavitshus, 1994, p. 1)

More than 40 years after independence, Ihonvbere (1997a, 1997b) stated that the stories of sub-Saharan African administrations consist of spectacular political, economic, and social failures. Those failures, he explained, have culminated in socioeconomic and political miseries for the African masses. The poor socioeconomic conditions of Africa prompted a former U.N. Secretary General to say that if steps were not taken to ameliorate the continent problem, Africa would stand the risk of becoming a lost continent. Several Western opinion leaders have called for the recolonization of Africa (Ayittey, 1997; Pfaff, 1995). Critics of American slavery and European economic, political, and human exploitation of the continent contend that, instead of being recolonized, African countries deserve reparation from the Europeans and Americans for the social problems they inflicted on the region (Chinweizu, 1993; Gifford, 1993).

In an article in *The Humanist*, Aronson (1993) quoted a French diplomat who said, "economically speaking, if the entire black Africa, with the exception of South Africa, were to disappear in a flood, the global cataclysm would be approximately nonexistent" (p. 9).

Singer and Wildavasky (1996) classified Africa as one of the regions with 85 percent of the world's population in the zones of turmoil and development, where "poverty, war, tyranny, and anarchy will continue to devastate lives" (p. 7). To overcome these problems, in the zones of turmoil and development, the authors contend that it will take about 100 years for most of the people in these areas to emerge from their economic, social, and political plights. They suggested that Africans have a long way to go to emerge from their economic, social, and political backwardness based on the existing economic conditions of Africa.

THE RISING PROMISE OF AFRICA IN
THE ERA OF GLOBALIZATION

Despite its pressing problems and challenges, Africa's economic prospects are improving. The continent has a population of more than 700 million people. With its population expected to double, reaching about 1.5 billion people within the first half of the twenty-first century, Africa promises to become a huge world marketplace as the number of potential customers continues to grow. However, if economic development does not keep pace with the increase in population, the increase may become a negative force and create social upheavals in the continent. Africa witnessed remarkable socioeconomic and political changes in the 1990s. In the realm of politics, Africa has seen the demise of authoritarian regimes. Efforts are being made to develop the continent's vast mineral resources to improve the welfare of their people. Corruption is being fought. Social economic indicators are rising. Debt relief programs and payments are being undertaken.

Africans are developing policies that rely on their values to reconstruct their part in development (De Beer, Kasoma, Megwa, & Steyn, 1995; Gaile & Ferguson, 1996; McGeary & Michaels, 1998).

As Africans struggle to improve their socioeconomic welfare, they have been warned to be cautious of their association with wealthy nations of the North in this era of globalization. Alleging that Europeans have posed more deadly threats to Africans than millions of wild beasts and mosquitoes, Eribo (2001) said that the Europeans have historically betrayed their sociocultural, economic, and political contacts and cooperation with Africa. Citing the Greek occupation of Alexandria, the Roman colonization of Numidia, the destruction of Carthage, the Trans-Atlantic Slave Trade, and decades of African colonization, Eribo said Europeans have always victimized Africans and other races with whom they have come in contact. Mamdani (1998) said that the creation of African states like the Congo are products of historical conquest designed to reproduce a European structure in Africa aimed at serving the economic interests of the powers that staged the Berlin conference of 1884/1885. The unnatural partition of Africa's natural boundaries helped the colonizers to maintain their colonial domination and contributed to the failure of African states since their independence.

However, addressing the Organization of African Unity (OAU) summit, Kofi Annan, the former United Nations Secretary-General, shifted the blame on Africans and African leaders for most of the continent's economic and political dispossessions, saying, "We have mismanaged our affairs for decades, and we are suffering from the accumulated effects" (Obadina, 2000). He added that:

> Africans have squandered development opportunities that underdeveloped nations in other regions of the Third World have grabbed to start pulling themselves out of mass poverty. Many African countries have unnecessarily entrapped themselves in a vicious cycle of conflict and poverty. The natural economic resources of the continent, particularly mineral deposits, have become major sources of corruption and strife, creating a no-win situation for ordinary Africans. (Obadina, 2000).

The former UN scribe said Africa is endowed with human and natural resources. Rather than using these resources to improve the welfare of the public, Annan decried the failure of African leaders who condemn their people to socioeconomic misery, stating that resources, instead of being exploited for the benefit of people, have been mismanaged and plundered so that they are now the source of our misery (Obadina, 2000).

Annan continued, "It is not unsurprising that African nations are being marginalized in this fast globalization world. African complaints that the rich world is not doing enough to assist in the continent's development are undermined by glaring evidence of the inability of African leaders to properly utilize aid" (Obadina, 2000). The United Nations chief called on African leaders to devise ways to help impoverished Africans without feeding the bloated stomachs of greedy corrupt leaders. During the 1990s, Africa experienced remarkable shifts in economic and political liberalization. President Thabo Mbeki of South Africa said Africans have chosen to redefine themselves through their actions because "Africans have grown tired of being told who they are, where they come from and where they ought to go and how they should proceed with their journey" (Asorock.com, 2001). He added that the reality is that the modern African has grown conscious and has "refused to be conditioned by circumstances imposed by a past of slavery, colonialism, neo-colonialism, racism and apartheid, has succeeded to create a new world of peace, democracy, development and prosperity" (Asorock.com, 2001).

President Mbeki said the emergence of the African Union and the New Partnership for Africa's Development constitute the mechanism that Africans have chosen to utilize their endowments to move the continent decisively forward toward a new realization of all the continent's past glory. However, he cautioned that the continent cannot continue on its progressive path and realize the necessary achievements if sections of the continent are engaged in wars, proliferation of weapons, religious fratricide, ethnic division, political intolerance, drug trafficking, and money laundering. He called on Africans to adopt policies that would stop the brain drain from Africa to other parts of the world.

Ali Mazrui, an eminent African historian, described Africa as a battleground for globalization. He cautioned African leaders to embrace globalization with care if the continent is to emerge from its socioeconomic woes. Mazrui said globalization might spell the final stage of annihilation of the continent if leaders do not rise to the challenges of the concept. Listing the dangers of globalization, he said its effects might be as devastating as that of slavery and colonialism on Africa (Anikulapo, 2001). He said that African leaders must become visionaries, wipe out corruption, and ignore wholesale adoption of Western values if the continent is to play a prominent role in the "villagization" process of the world that globalization portends.

Mbeki and Mazrui's pleas and observations are in keeping with the visions of Kwame Nkrumah, Ghana's first prime minister, who strategized that Africans must join forces through pan-Africanism if they are to achieve and return to their past greatness. During a meeting of the Organization of African Unity, Kwame Nkrumah, Ghana's first prime minister, offered his vision, based on his Pan-Africanist ideals, of what he believed Africa could promote for the welfare of her masses when he said:

If we are to remain free, if we are to enjoy the full benefits of Africa's rich resources, we must unite, to plan for our total defense and the full exploitation of our material and human means, in the full interests of our people. "To go it alone" will limit our horizons, curtail our expectations, and threaten our liberty. (Ward, 1989, p. 55)

Kenneth Meshoe, the leader of the African Democratic Party in South Africa, echoed similar sentiments, saying:

For this vision to become a reality, firm commitments have to be made by all stakeholders to good governance, democracy, the rule of law, human rights, fiscal discipline and accountability. All African leaders who are part of this new partnership must hold one another accountable. They must understand that although the ideal situation would be equal benefits for all partners, the reality would be different. There must be equal dedication and effort from all role-players to make the new partnership work. (Asorock.com, 2001)

In May 2001, the Organization of African Unity changed its name to African Union to forge closer economic, sociocultural, and political ties (Ebonugwo & Ogbeifun, 2001). During the past 30 years, several regional trade blocs have been formed. These include Southern African Development Community (SADC), Common Market of East and Southern African States (COMESA), East African Community (EAC), The Arab Maghreb Union (AMU), Economic Community of Central African States (ECCAS), and the 16-member Economic Community of West African States (ECOWAS). ECOWAS has a population of more than 210 million. Formed in 1975, the aims of ECOWAS, like those in other regions of Africa, are:

To promote cooperation and development in all fields of industry, transport, telecommunication, energy, agriculture, natural resources, commerce, monetary and financial questions and in social and cultural matters for the purpose of raising the standard of living of its peoples. (Fadeiye, 1978, p. 81)

DEBATE ON SOCIAL DEVELOPMENT AND COMMUNICATION DEVELOPMENT

Haque (1993) said the growing attention given to development or modernization has turned the concept into a global "civil religion." As with any religious debate, there is a great gulf among what development entails, how it has been or should be pursued, and what vehicle(s) should be used to achieve the goal of transforming the Third World. As the debate rages, scholars are now asking two key questions: Does development exclusively entail the transformation of people in a society from a lower economic status to a higher and better economic condition as Western dogma postulates (Opubor, 1986)? Or is development a process concerned with a broader array of issues that range from sociocultural to economic freedom and human opportunities of health, education, creativity, and the enjoyment of self-respect and human rights as Third World societies believe (Isar, 1996)?

Having witnessed the accelerated transformation of Western societies from Agricultural, Industrial, and Nuclear revolutions to the Information Age, Third World societies are emulating the West and are working hard to catch up. Thus, it could be argued that the Western view has won because every measure of development is based on Western experience and its reliance on economic measurements and indices. Inayatullah (1976) disagreed. He said that Western models of development have failed the Third World and are thus undesirable as modalities for implementing their socioeconomic development because they attribute underdevelopment to traditional forces alone while absolving external forces such as consumerism, colonialism, and global economic marginalization. Sen (1996) said that the reliance on economic indices only is misleading and presents a false picture because human existence entails more than economic prosperity. He contended that development is concerned with cultural affinity, spiritual growth, and self-determination.

As the Information Age, which Marshall McLuhan predicted during the first half of the twentieth century, has dawned, the debate about the role of technology in human development has taken center stage. The Information Age has been described as a period when dependence on information will become the mainstay of the world economy (Whetmore, 1995). It marks a period based on service instead of manufacturing when a majority of the labor force will be employed to produce, manufacture, and retrieve information and data with computers. It has been suggested that acquiring and employing ICTs has the potential to assist developing nations to transform their economies from backwardness into modern states. In a nutshell, technological advocates claim that ICTs promise a utopian society, where the lack of food, water, shelter, clothing, and access to information will cease to exist, and plagues such as famine, drought, infant mortality, epidemics, and war will be healed. These transformations and promises will be fulfilled because ICTs will enable developing nations to operate a knowledge-based economy.

This prediction and promise are not new. Third World leaders and development planners have been aware of these potential breakthroughs for more than 50 years. Western scholars who recommended and prescribed information have advocated the view that ICTs remain the vehicles that will enable developing nations to sail out of their economic abyss into economic prosperity (Lerner, 1963). This dogma has been described as "social construction." Social constructionists contend that human and societal needs dictate the course of technological innovations, and that technological changes could be directed and used to benefit humanity and its developing societies. This view is contradicted by "technological determinism" (Hughes, 2000).

Technological determinists view technology and technological innovations as independent forces outside human control, and they claim that they dictate and influence the course of human and societal developments. Hughes (2000) offers a third concept—technological momentum. Technological momentum is based on the notion that "newer, developing systems {technologies} are generally more open to societal influences than more mature developing systems, which are more resistant to external influences and thus more deterministic" (p. 26). African experiences with technologies as vehicles for social modernization and economic development remain unclear and uncharted.

Despite the lack of clarity and any clear course, Bourgault (1995) said that African administrations and other governments in the developing world had long recognized, invested, and developed their mass media and telecommunications infrastructures as vehicles to be used for political, economic, cultural, and social mobilization of their countries and their peoples (Moemeka, 1994; Ngugi, 1995; Ziegler & Asante, 1992). Since adopting ICTs as vehicles for promoting development and modernization in the Third World, there have been conflicting views about their applications and contributions to social development. This is because the promises made more than half a century ago remain unfruitful (McNelly, 1968). Studies have demonstrated an insignificant relationship between communication and national development. Despite the lack of success, Western scholars and their supporters (such as the United Nations) have continued to prescribe ICTs as the panacea for lifting developing nations into moderately or developed nations (Uche, 1988, 1994, 1997). They contend they remain a force that will transport the developing world out of the zone of turmoil and stagnant development where poverty, war, tyranny, and anarchy plague its existence.

African and other Third World leaders and development planners still cling to that hope and still stretch their hands to collect the Manna ICTs' promise. However, as a result of the failure of information and communication development to deliver, 30 years have passed since some degree of skepticism has developed about the capability of telecommunications to assist with the transformation of developing nations (Rogers, 1976). Despite the skepticism, information and communication are still being promoted and relied on to promote modernization in the Third World (Uche, 1988, 1994, 1997). Considering this contradiction, one question begs for an answer with regard to technological determinism in Africa in this era of technological explosion and globalization: Are African societies driven by technologies or are technologies driving African societies?

AFRICA AND THE DEBATE ON ACQUISITION OF TECHNOLOGY AND TELECOMMUNICATION

To address the preceding question, another question comes to mind: Should nations in sub-Saharan Africa invest heavily in ICTs to join the Information

Age as quickly as possible? Or should they invest moderately in these technologies to allocate their scarce resources to deal with the vexing economic and sociocultural problems plaguing the continent? Wacieni (1996) said that the per capita GNP of people in sub-Saharan Africa stands at $365, whereas the per capita debt averaged $334. This has produced a staggering debt to the GNP ratio of 91 percent. At the end of 1997, the amount of debt that African countries owed Western institutions ranged from $215 to $225 billion. Most Africans survive on less than a dollar a day (Aziken, 2001). If Africans rely on such limited resources, one is prompted to ask why and what resources they have to commit to any technology.

Of all the world's regions, Africa has the poorest information and communication infrastructures. Thus, the need far exceeds the government financing capacity. Here lies the core debate about the digital divide. There are three schools of thought on this subject. The first school views technology as an "unalloyed blessing" for social development. This school claims that technology promotes progress and prosperity, provides solutions to social problems, and liberates humanity from complex and highly organized society (Hughes, 2000). This perspective also contends that African nations and other Third World countries should invest heavily in communication infrastructures because to do so will help them to move quickly into the future. This view argues that information technology promotes openness, access, networking, and problem solving that transform societies and bring people together. Proponents say that information technology is not an exotic venture that caters to the residents or transnational corporations of developed nations. Rather, it should be viewed as a vehicle for Third World nations to stimulate economic growth, provide employment, and enhance productivity and welfare of their peoples (Uche, 1988, 1994, 1997).

The second school contends that technology remains an "unmitigated curse" on humanity that has robbed people of their dignity, jobs, privacy, democratic participation, and religious beliefs (Hughes, 2000). They argue that technology promotes materialism and a technocratic society where a few elite and foreign concerns dominate. This school of thought contends that African governments should not invest heavily in technology because technological breakthroughs that were achieved outside the continent have harmed Africa. They argue that Africa should invest in programs that fight the scourge of poverty, illiteracy, diseases, and conflicts. This group contends that, since the Middle Ages, imported technologies have had an adverse impact on Africa. They point out that the advent of ocean exploration helped the Europeans to dominate, colonize, and enslave Africans. They further argue that the Agricultural Revolution lifted Europeans from poverty and starvation, but contributed to the enslavement of Africans. This group claims that the Industrial Revolution accelerated the pace of industrial development, but enabled the Europeans to conquer the continent and to exploit their natural resources without substantial investment in Africa. They claim that the West has used its technological superiority to undermine African value systems (Nyamnjoh, 1999; Ziegler & Asante, 1992).

The third school propounds a moderate view. Adherents believe that humanity has gained experience from the technological revolutions of the past, hence technological breakthroughs do not deserve the special attention they used to command. They argue that most of the technologies developed in the last 50 years have not been as traumatic as earlier technological revolutions because the levels of education and sophistication have closed the gap between invention and adoption. They claim that technological breakthroughs have not necessarily accelerated the rate of economic development (Hughes, 2000). This school of thought contends that information technology should not be viewed as the panacea of African social and economic problems. They contend that investment in information technology should be driven by socioanthropological needs. This will enable these societies to maintain some degree of control over information and disseminated content that is useful and relevant for their needs (Bentsi-Enchill, 1999).

THE DIGITAL DIVIDE: STATUS OF AFRICA

Of the four main technologies (electricity, telephone, satellite, and computer) that drive the current revolution in ICTs, Africa remains dismally behind in the development of these technologies. As stated earlier, Africa's population is estimated to be more than 700 million (12 percent of the world's population), of which about 470 million reside in sub-Saharan Africa. More than 70 percent live in rural areas, and more than 80 percent of Africa's rural areas do not have electricity (Ngwainmbi, 1999).

In 1994, it was estimated that the world had more than 703 million telephone access points, which included 648 million fixed lines and 55 million wireless cellular lines. The continent had 14 million telephone lines. Africa's teledensity (the number of telephone lines per 100 residents) remains poor and is estimated to be 1.66. Between 1994 and 1995, the International Telecommunication Union (ITU) estimated Africa's teledensity varied from 0.08 in Chad to .0.46 in Nigeria and other nations in sub-Saharan Africa. North African teledensity is estimated to be 4.22. Of this marginal number, it is estimated that 50 percent of the lines in Africa are in urban areas, where less than 30 percent of the people reside. There are about 2.5 and 10 lines per 1,000 people in East and West Africa. Sahelian and Central African countries have fewer than 2 lines per 1,000 residents, while North and South Africa have 30 lines per 1,000 residents (about 1 line per 50 people). Fewer than 1 in 50 Africans have direct telephone lines. Africans spend about $400 million to route their calls to Europe or the United States. The average annual growth of lines in Africa is about 10 percent, with more than 1 million people on a waiting list for a phone.

There is one public telephone for every 7,000 people in Africa. The world's ratio is 1 per 600. There are three computers for every 1,000 Africans. One in every 1,500 Africans has access to the Internet, whereas the world's rate is about 1 in 40. Africa has about 3 million Internet users, with about 1 million outside South Africa (i.e., 1 Internet user per 250 people).

Internet providers are concentrated in national capitals or commercial cities. They are almost nonexistent in rural areas. The average cost of an Internet account for 5 hours a month is about $60. The average in developed nations is $18. Africa generates only .4 percent of the contents of the World Wide Web. The current estimated number of computers permanently connected to the Internet in Africa ranges from 25,000 to 35,000 (for details on the status of African telecommunication technologies, see *Africa Recovery*, 1999a; Jensen, 1998, 2000; Mbendi, 1997; Neal, 1998; Ngwainmbi, 1999;). Until the early 1990s, sub-Saharan Africa remained the only part of the world without a regional satellite of its own (Boafo, 1991).

Since the colonial era, when communication technologies (radio, TV, print, film, advertising, and public relations) were introduced into Africa, the continent has been dependent on Japan, Europe, and the United States for hardware and software. It has also been dependent on the West for technical assistance and financing. Transnational corporations dominate advertising and public relations. This dependence on developed nations by the Third World has led to accusations of cultural imperialism because of the imbalance of the flow of software from developed to developing nations. This lack of balance also has prompted calls for New World Information and Communication Order (NWIO). The concept calls for increased effort to enhance the flow of information technology and content from the South to the North. The goal of this concept is to correct the current situation where information content dominantly flows from the North to the South. It should be noted that when communication technologies were introduced, the colonial masters used them as vehicles to control and exploit the masses and to provide home news for white colonial officials. Mass media were used to undermine traditional values while promoting Western culture and domination (Boafo, 1991; De Beer, Kasoma, Megwa, & Steyn, 1995; Ziegler & Asante, 1992).

After independence, African leaders cloned the style of colonial officials and authoritarian regimes and have been using government-controlled mass media as the driving force to perpetuate power in the guise of promoting economic development and national integration. During the last decade, many African governments have liberalized their governments' communication policies. With the entry of private outlets, mass media are becoming increasingly freer and competitive. Television can hardly be described as a mass medium in Africa because only the affluent can afford it. Print is mostly consumed by the educated and affluent. Radio has been described as the democratic media because it is more affordable and reaches the largest number of people. Mass media outlets in Africa are concentrated in the urban areas. Most African nations use obsolete communication technologies because they lack the resources to maintain existing technologies or to purchase new ones. They are largely dependent on analog technologies. Digital technologies are being introduced at a snail's pace (Boafo, 1991; De Beer, Kasoma, Megwa, & Steyn, 1995; Ngwainmbi, 1999).

DIGITAL DIVIDE: WHY IT EXISTS IN AFRICA

Sub-Saharan Africa has the least developed communication ICTs and infrastructures. Based on studies conducted in ECOWAS nations, including Nigeria, Ghana, Benin, Senegal, and other countries in sub-Saharan Africa, several key factors have been blamed for creating the digital divide. The inadequate financial resources of African countries have been fingered as the leading culprit. The International Telecommunication Union (ITU) estimates that it will cost $50 billion to make African telecommunication competitive with other regions by providing five telephones per 100 Africans (Neal, 1998). At this rate, countries in sub-Saharan Africa lack the financial resources to initiate sustainable information and communication infrastructures without assistance from developed nations and world institutions. Without this assistance, Africa will remain an observer as other developing regions of the South take the voyage into the Information Age, where the North has already landed. It is estimated that the cost of phone connection in Africa's largely low-income countries hovered at 20 percent of the continent's per capita gross domestic income in 1995, compared with 1 percent in high-income countries (*Africa Recovery*, 1999b).

Obtrusive government policies and strict regulations also have been cited as factors contributing to the digital divide. In many African countries, governments control the telecommunications sector. They are operated inefficiently. Competition and investments from the private sector are discouraged. In recent years, several countries, including Ivory Coast, Senegal, Nigeria, and Ghana, have partially or fully privatized their telecommunications sector. These countries suffer from insufficient interest on the part of local and international private sector organizations to invest in developing technology infrastructures and establishing communication and information services (*Africa Recovery*, 1999b; Ministry of Communications—Ghana, 2001). Investors may believe the level of economic development in African countries could hinder their ability to generate profit. The lack of coordination within key ministries in African countries and inadequate collaboration among African governments (Francophone and Anglophone countries) stifle the development of ICTs in sub-Saharan Africa (*Africa Recovery*, 1999b).

Most of the ECOWAS countries and other nations in sub-Saharan Africa lack modern and updated telecommunication infrastructures based on digital technology. These countries are minimally capable of international connections because of insufficient bandwidth. They have inadequate teledensity and computers (i.e., the number of telephone lines or personal computers per 100 inhabitants). Most are plagued with a poor level of computer literacy and unavailability of training (Ministry of Communications—Ghana, 2001).

The public interest in services offered by private providers remains inadequate. This might be due to high cost. It costs an average of $50 to use a local dial-up Internet account for 5 hours a month. However, the charges for Internet services vary greatly between $10 and $1,000 depending on the maturity of markets, tariff policies of the telecom operators, national policies, and access to international telecommunications bandwidth. Compounding the lack of interest is the unwillingness among Africans to change their traditional habits—oral communication and trepidation to move from the known to the unknown. About 1 million Africans subscribed to Internet service providers (Ministry of Communications—Ghana, 2001).

SUGGESTIONS FOR BRIDGING THE DIVIDE

As with most news emanating from Africa, the news dealing with the digital divide has been negative and has occupied an appreciable amount of space in the global news media. This alarm has caused many international organizations and nongovernment agencies, as well as governments in and outside Africa, to commission studies to discern how the gap can be closed. These studies have involved ECOWAS nations and other countries in sub-Saharan Africa; many solutions are being proffered and will be explored. Based on feasibility studies conducted by the African Information Society, efforts to close the digital divide consist of four components: (a) institutional, policy, framework, and legal, regulatory, and management mechanism; (b) human resource development; (c) information resources and content; and (d) technological resources and infrastructure (Economic Commission for Africa, 1998).

Institutional, Policy, Framework, and Legal, Regulatory, and Management Mechanism

Institutional framework calls for collaboration among different stakeholders. The collaboration should be conducted among the government, the private sector, nongovernmental groups, and community-based groups. Governments must provide leadership in establishing and facilitating mechanisms for other participants. They must adopt policies and legal framework and develop institutions that provide direction for companies with interest in the development of the information and communication sector. As a result, government policies should be geared toward the development of the local digital services and products, protection of the local information technology industry, and eradication of current disparities in information access among various sectors of the society. They should engage in human resource development. Governments should also examine the impact of technology and globalization with regard to the protection of intellectual property rights, the licensing of information providers, the right of access to free information, flow of transboarder information, and the affordability and availability of information the public sector generates.

To attain these goals, governments must adopt evolving policies and legislative frameworks that will continue to facilitate the introduction and maintenance of ICTs[.] As ICTs become increasingly critical for economic development, several governments, including Nigeria, Ghana, and Senegal, have liberalized their telecommunication sectors. These countries are hoping that liberalization will enhance the development of ICTs. Nigeria is setting up an independent agency to regulate the national telecommunications sector.

Human Resource Development

Without the development of the human capacity to use information services and professionals to create and maintain these facilities, the African information sector will remain constrained. Recognizing this fact, efforts to develop a sustainable information sector compel African governments to initiate strategic plans for national educational training programs. This can be achieved on two levels. The first calls for establishing research and development to build knowledge and create and implement relevant infrastructure and technologies. The second level calls for stable training programs in schools, churches, and businesses to train women, community leaders, and youth in urban and rural communities. Professionals, policymakers, and information technology experts should be encouraged to undertake training. Some strides are being made in this arena. Training programs are springing up all over Africa. Ghana represents a good case where foreign assistance has helped to train technicians to maintain information and communication infrastructures. The United Nations and supranationals are contributing to the training of Africans. African governments are encouraged to find ways to curtail the brain drain in the information technology sector by providing incentives for locally trained professionals to remain in the continent. They should also tap the talents and services of Africans in the Diaspora (Davidson, 1999).

Information Resources

This topic is concerned with content and application. Africans generate less than 1 percent of the content on the Internet, and most of that information is not accessible to Africans. To address this imbalance, African governments are encouraged to place priorities by generating content on education, health, electronic government service delivery, and commerce. They are taking adequate steps to ensure that the masses have access to affordable service. The issue of content is important. If Africa is to benefit from ICTs, then content available to the public must reflect their needs. This content should address economic and sociocultural subjects. Most of the content on the Internet that Africans access originates from the West. Content is entertainment-oriented and laden with foreign values. Critics are clamoring that the Internet is rapidly becoming a tool for imperialism. Literacy remains low in Africa. This poses challenges for experts developing content. They must find unique ways to develop content that the public can access and find useful for their needs.

Technological Resources and Infrastructure

Most African countries have poor information and communication infrastructures. To foster the development of infrastructure, African governments are advised to liberalize their telecommunications industry to allow competition and private investment. Offering tax incentives and loans to private investors may help with the development of infrastructures. Governments are also encouraged to form partnerships with local and international technology to acquire, install, and maintain ICTs in urban and rural communities. To accomplish this goal, governments are urged to introduce the private sector to multipurpose telecommunication centers that provide Internet, telephone, fax, and information services. Although some efforts are being made in this regard, the lack of financial resources remains a hindrance. However, privatization is creating and exacerbating unemployment problems in the Third World. As telecommunications become privatized, government workers in the telecommunications industry are being displaced. Government-owned telecommunications agencies employ a huge number of workers in most developing nations. Increased privatization has led to greater unemployment.

PAST AND CURRENT PROJECTS AIMED AT BRIDGING THE GAP

Of the 151,000 villages in Africa, about 122,000 (80 percent of the continent's population) have no telephone or electricity. It requires about 4 million telephone lines at a cost of almost $6 billion to provide one telephone line per 150 Africans (Ngwainmbi, 1999).

Despite these daunting challenges, Balit (1996) said that African governments are keenly aware of the importance of ICTs as vehicles for promoting their policies and development programs. She says that the role and place of ICTs in developmental policies have become an item of high priority for most African governments and a subject of intellectual debate. She emphasizes that the need for communication policies to help with development must be "planned systematically, implemented and coordinated" to yield an effective outcome. With the assistance of the United Nations, its agencies, nongovernmental organizations, international agencies, and several foreign governments, countries in sub-Saharan Africa have undertaken initiatives to develop information and communication infrastructures in the region. For example, just 3 years after its formation in 1975, the ECOWAS Council of Ministers recommended and the Authority of the Heads of State approved the Community Telecommunication program known as the International Telecommunication Company (INTELCOM I). The principal objectives of the program were outlined as follows:

- To open Member States that do not have reliable links to the outsider world.
- To complete the missing links in the PANAFTEL network in West Africa.
- To increase telecommunication traffic within ECOWAS nations. (ECOWAS Official Site, 2001)

Having met about 95 percent of these goals, ECOWAS launched INTELCOM II, which was aimed at providing the community "with a regional telecommunication network that is modern, reliable, and capable of offering a wider variety of services including multi-media and wide band services . . . " (ECOWAS Official Site, 2001). The ITU is providing $222,000 to fund this second phase (Ikeh, 1999). Pratt (1996) said that for the past three decades, African regions have used a variety of means to acquire new technologies to assist in attaining sustained development. Some of these efforts include the establishment of the Pan-African Telecommunication Network (PANTEL), Regional African Satellite Communication System (RASCOM), and Southern African Development Coordination and Conference Telecommunication Network (SADCC). They also have sought the services of Washington, DC-based International Telecommunication Satellite Organization (INTELSAT) and London-based International Maritime Satellite Organization (INMARSAT).

Recognizing the economic plight of Africa, in 1996, the United Nations launched a Special Initiative on Africa aimed at marshaling the resources of every arm of the organization to direct $25 billion toward African social and economic development over 10 years (United Nations/Economic Commission for Africa, 1998). In May 1995, 53 African ministers of social and economic development and planning asked the United Nations/Economic Commission for Africa to initiate a high-level working group on ICTs in Africa. The ministers asked to establish the working group to produce a report that would design strategies and policies African nations should adopt to acquire and utilize the resources of the ICTs. After year-long studies and a series of meetings, the group produced a framework document entitled "Africa Information

Society Initiative (AISI): An Action Framework to Build Africa's Information and Communication Infrastructure," which calls for

> The elaboration of and implementation of national information and communication infrastructure plans involving development of institutional frameworks, human, information and technological resources in all African countries and the pursuit of priority strategies, programs and projects which can assist in the sustainable build-up of an information society in African countries. (Africa Information Society Initiative, 2001)

The document was submitted to ministers at the 22nd meeting of the Economic Commission for Africa in May 1996. At the meeting, African planning ministers adopted Resolution 812, entitled Implementation of the African Information Society Initiative (AISI).

The ministers agreed that ICTs will help African countries to speed up development plans, stimulate growth, increase trade, create jobs, and provide new opportunities for delivering education, health care, and food (Africa Information Society Initiative, 2001; Jensen, 2000). Economic Community for Africa reports that there are about 1,000 externally funded information and communication projects being undertaken in Africa, and about 22 African countries are at different stages of devising and implementing plans for a national information communication infrastructure. The aim of these revisions is to acquire and use telecommunication technology at national and sectoral levels (*Africa Recovery*, 1999b).

The United Nations, a long-term advocate of the use of ICTs to assist the Third World's modernization to enable it to avoid the early stages of development and to raise the standard of living, provided about $11.5 million to launch the African Information Society Program and to build new ICTs as part of its 1996 Special Initiative on Africa (Jensen, 2000). Forty African communication ministers have endorsed the initiative, and a goal has been set to establish an African Connection Telecenter in all 52 African states. These Telecenters will serve as a forum where Africans can share their experiences and research on the impact of ICTs in their countries. ECOWAS member states that have begun to use the initiative to transform their information and communication infrastructure include Benin and Burkina Faso. It is hoped that these countries will share their experiences with other member and nonmember states. Since the mid-1990s, several projects have been undertaken to enhance the information and communication infrastructure and accessibility in Africa (*Africa Recovery*, 1999a, 1999b, 1999c; Jensen, 2000; Mwaura, 1998; Neal, 1998). These include:

- The U.S. Agency for International Development/Leland Initiative's
- AfricaLink, which aims to build Internet connectivity in 20 African countries in exchange for liberalizing the market for private providers. Ghana and Guinea represent

- ECOWAS in this initiative. The project calls for collaboration with public and private agencies from the United States.
- The International Telecommunication Union (ITU) is involved in various rural, community, and satellite projects with other agencies like World Health Organization (WHO) and UNESCO.
- The World Bank is assisting in the development of information and telecommunication facilities in 25 countries. The Bank's assistance is contingent on African governments embarking on privatization of their telecommunication industry and the involvement of the private sector. One of the major initiatives is the establishment of African Virtual University (allows a course to be conducted online).
- UNESCO has established the Creating Learning Network for African Teachers project to assist teacher-training colleges to develop literacy in information science.
- The project has started in Senegal. With funding from Italy and the Netherlands, UNESCO has implemented and established the Regional Informatic Network for Africa. The United Nations Conference on Trade and Development's TradePoints has established initiatives for developing efficiency networks in Africa.
- With a sum of $6 million, the United Nations Development Program's (UNDP) African Bureau has embarked on an Internet Initiative for Africa. The program is aimed at improving Internet connectivity. ECOWAS members engaged in this program include Nigeria, Burkina Faso, Gambia, and Togo. UNDP's Sustainable Development Networking Program has established 10 operation nodes in Africa. ECOWAS member states engaged in the project include Benin and Togo.
- The United Nations Environment Program's Mercure project has introduced a program using Very Small Aperture Terminal (VSAT) information technology to establish an environmental information exchange network in Africa.
- Agence de la Francophonie and related international agencies have initiated various programs to develop information and communication technologies in Africa.
- In 1996, only 11 African countries had Internet access, but by November 2000, most countries had achieved permanent connectivity.

THE NIGERIAN TECHNOLOGY POLICY

Nigerian technology experts report that poor economic/acquisition cost, poor technology infrastructure, lack of sociocultural/education and awareness, and poor government regulations and payment systems are the major barriers to the development of the nation's information and communication technology, which has adversely affected the growth of the economy

(Ebhodaghe, 2001, Jan. 30). To escape from the current snail pace in the growth of the information and technology sector, the experts agree that there must be:

- an increase in private sector initiatives;
- government support and encouragement;
- government policy changes, liberalization of government control, and the breaking of monopolies;
- creation of a conducive environment for strategic investors to invest in Nigeria; a reduction of import duties on IT equipment and related accessories should be reduced;
- more venture capital and firms to provide funding for e-commerce project development;
- create greater of awareness in the population of the benefits of e-commerce; and
- a gradual changing of society from a cash to a cashless economy.

- (Ebhodaghe, 2001, Jan. 30).

Reacting to these concerns, the federal government set up a presidential panel to develop a framework for a national Information Technology (IT) policy. The panel issued a report that it hoped would "make Nigeria an information technology superpower in Africa, and a key player in the information society by the year 2006," and "to position the country as a technologically active nation and key player in the information age, using software as the engine for development, sustainable growth and global competitiveness" (Ebhodaghe, 2001, Feb. 20). The report, largely adopted by the federal government, establishes the Nigeria Information Communication Technology (ICT) policy. The policy, which has a 31-point-objective, includes the following concepts:

- to ensure that information technology resources are readily available for national development toward providing solutions to the challenges of the Information Age;
- to reengineer and improve urban and rural development, and to enhance planning mechanisms and forecasting for the development of local infrastructure and environmental monitoring and control;
- to improve health care delivery system, food production, and food security, and to empower children, women, and the disabled by providing special programs that will promote IT diffusion in all sectors of national life;
- to enhance national security and law enforcement to endeavor to bring the defense and law enforcement agencies in line with accepted best practices in the national interest and to strengthen national identity and unity;

- to stimulate the private sector as a driving force for IT creativity, enhanced productivity and competitiveness and also to establish new multifaceted IT institutions as centers of excellence to ensure Nigeria's competitiveness in international markets;
- to create Special Incentive Programmes (SIPs) to induce investment in IT sector and to generate additional foreign exchange earnings through expanded indigenous IT products and services; and
- to develop human capital with emphasis on creating and supporting a knowledgebased society and to build a pool of IT literate manpower using the National Youth Service Corp (NYSC) and other platforms as "train the trainer scheme" (TTT) for capacity building. (Ebhodaghe, 2001, Feb. 20).

Among the strategies the government hopes to employ to achieve the objectives are the following:

- establishing a coordinated program for the development of a National Information Infrastructure (NII), State Information Infrastructure (SII), and Local Information Infrastructure (LII) backbone by providing emerging technologies such as satellite, including Very Small Aperture Terminal (VSAT), fiber optic networks, high-speed gateways, and broad band/multimedia, and providing adequate connectivity to the Global Information Infrastructure (GII);
- addressing open standards for further liberalization and the fiscal measures, including incentives to substantially improve teledensity and make IT more affordable to the citizenry;
- establishing IT parks as incubating centers for the development of software applications at national, state, and local levels. Encouraging massive local and global IT skills acquisitions through training in the public and private sectors with the view to achieving a strategic medium-term milestone of at least 500,000 IT skilled personnel by the year 2004;
- restructuring the education system at all levels to respond effectively to the challenges and imagined impact of the Information Age and, in particular, the allocation of a special IT development fund to education at all levels;
- restructuring health care by providing a national databank to provide online national health care information and administration and management at primary, secondary, and tertiary level(s);
- establishing national IT awareness machinery at all levels of government and encouraging private sector participation in exposing Nigerians to the use and benefits of IT, with a view to strengthening the government's and private sector's collaboration for the attainment of self-reliance;
- creating national database management systems as tools for effective planning and communication between citizens at home and abroad and to enhance defense and law enforcement;

- bringing the government to the doorsteps of people by creating a virtual forum and facilities to strengthen accessibility to government information and facilitating interaction between the governed and government, leading to transparency, accountability, and the strengthening of democracy; and
- utilizing IT opportunities to restructure government, citizens, and business interfaces or better governance, improved trade and commerce, and administrative effectiveness. (Ebhodaghe, 2001, Feb. 20).

To achieve the short- to medium-term objectives of this policy with maximum effectiveness, the policy calls on the government to establish a National IT Development Agency (NITDA) to implement, monitor, evaluate, and verify progress via an ongoing basis under the supervision and coordination of the Federal Ministry of Science and Technology. The policy further states that the government should also ensure an adequate National Information Technology Development and Intervention Fund (NITDIF) to achieve the short- to medium-term objectives of the policy by earmarking in the first instance, at least 5 percent of the national budget to implement the policy thrust and compel all ministries and parastatals to do the same.

The identified specific core areas that are expected to benefit from the new policy include:

- Agriculture: The policy hopes to use IT to reengineer agriculture for the purpose of maximizing food production, improving food self-sufficiency and security, increasing output for industrial raw material generation, providing employment and economic growth, and minimizing environmental abuse and degradation. To achieve these goals, the nation shall develop a Geographical Information System (GIS) to monitor the environment and planned sustainable environmental usage. Agricultural extension services will be equipped to help farmers in areas of digital mapping, soil types, ecology, and creating special IT awareness for all types of farmers at all levels among others.
- Trade, Commerce, and Finance: Here, the policy hopes to create an enabling environment that empowers stakeholders in trade and commerce with the underlying infrastructure to improve productivity and positively position the nation for global competition to positively raise the local and international visibility of Nigerian businesses. To achieve this goal, the import duty on IT components and software tools, for industries set up for the sole purpose of exporting of finished IT products and services will be duty-free, whereas import duties on IT components and any software for the domestic market will be 1 percent, whereas import duties on imported finished IT goods for the domestic market will be 7 percent. (Ebhodaghe, 2001, Feb. 20)

The Minister of State for Science and Technology, Pauline Tallen, said the policy provides the country with a road map for a sector that has operated without adequate coordination in consonance with the objective for improving the economic welfare of the masses (Ayeoyenikan, 2001). This statement demonstrates that the government responded positively to the report and may take steps to implement the recommendations in the near future.

A CALL FOR "BALANCED ACTION"

As African leaders and development planners embark on various programs to acquire ICTs, they must be advised to consider the prevailing economic conditions in their countries and base their efforts on established African values as they relate to technology. They should not rush, but proceed cautiously. At the apex of black civilization, about 6,000 years ago, Africans created, introduced, and relied on the basic disciplines of human knowledge: science, technology, geometry, mathematics, logic, medicine, ethics, and architecture. The recent discovery of an 8,000-year-old canoe in Dafuna, Yobe State Nigeria, attests to African technical ingenuity in transportation and other forms of communication (*The Guardian Online*, 2001, April 19). African technical creativity underscores useful and nondestructive inventions (Katembo, 2001).

This is because Africans have always depended on nature for their livelihood. African value systems do not view nature as a force that must be subdued, but as a force that must be nurtured and cooperated with to maintain a balance between nature and humans who exploit its resources for their livelihood. This relationship with nature compelled Africans to adopt a technological concept known as *sociotechnology*. Katembo (2001) said the purpose of sociotechnology is to "improve the quality of life in villages and other living spaces"; thus, the concept represents "the purposeful use of knowledge and information in the areas of science, economics and materials to address the needs of people from a physical perspective" (p. 2).

This exploration, which examined the role and development of ICTs in sub-Saharan Africa, is aimed at advocating a balanced action as the course African nations should adopt in their quest to build communication infrastructures to assist national development. A balanced action constitutes six elements and requires African governments to (a) avoid foreign loans and spend only a fraction of their annual budgets (within 5 to 10 percent if possible) on acquiring ICTs; (b) liberalize their policies and encourage privatization in the telecommunications industry in a manner beneficial to everyone in a society, not only to societal elites; (c) build and rely on simple tools to work on the existing infrastructure and evolve higher technologies on a step-by-step basis; (d) concentrate on providing public access in rural areas, community centers, and institutions; (e) rely on contents and applications developed in Africa that are socioanthropologically driven to deal with the daunting tasks facing the continent; and (f) encourage research that will help to discern areas of technical and sociocultural needs and applications, as well as areas of training to maintain the infrastructures and teach the masses how to use these technologies.

Examining the proposed Nigerian ICT policy, it could be argued that the proposal includes some elements advocated, but due consideration can only take place when the proposal is implemented. If Nigerian and other African governments adopt the "balanced action model," they will be keeping with African traditional cultural values and the concept of sociotechnology (Katembo, 2001). Mali's President Alpha Oumar Konare captured the essence of the model when he stated: "As an African, I am keeping a cool head—a computer can cost eighty years' salary or send 20 children to school . . . If we don't have our own clear vision on information and communication technology, we will be disappointed. . . . We must not fall into the trap of separating our cultural (experience) from economic development. Globalization is inevitable but we have to enter it while being true to ourselves" (Bentsi-Enchill, 1999).

Thus, this study advocates a "Balanced Action" model as the mechanism that nations in sub-Saharan Africa might utilize in their quest to adopt information technology and to join the global economy. The model will assist with economic and sociocultural transformation of these societies and enhance the welfare of their masses without aggravating the fragile and desperate situation on the continent as critics contended when Nigerian launched telecommunication satellites (Raufu, 2003). Considering the developing status of these nations, the object of this model is to offer a mechanism that these and other developing nations may adopt as a realistic approach to acquire information technology and to compete in the world economy without neglecting other aspects of sociocultural development.

7 Manifestations of Meanings and Cultural Values in Advertising

ADVERTISING MESSAGES AND MEANING

The past four decades have witnessed a growing scholarly interest in examining the role and practice of advertising with regard to the sociocultural, political, developmental, and regulatory issues surrounding the medium in today's global and technological economic contexts within and across cultures and societies in an increasingly interdependent world (Cheng, 1997; Lin, 2001; Stafford, 2005; Zandpour et al., 1994).

Cheng (1997) noted that most of the cross-cultural studies on advertising have focused on the comparison of Western cultures or on Eastern and Western cultures. Few have been conducted that compare the values present in advertising with that of African cultural values (Al-Olayan & Karande, 2000; Harris & Attour, 2000). The growing importance and interest on the subject could be attributed to increased and vociferous debate over the role of advertising in developing societies in an increasingly interdependent global economy, where ICTs have made the transfer of information and mass media artifacts like advertising across boarders rapid, constant, and accessible. In a global economy where ICTs are playing a growing role, proponents of advertising described advertising as an economic ingredient that lubricates the capitalism, the world dominant economic system. Others view advertising as a vast economic wasteland that demeans traditional values and promotes consumerism, especially in the developing world in this era of globalization (Frith & Mueller, 2003; Arens, 2004; Alozie, 2004; Pollay and Gallagher, 1990). Proponents and detractors of advertising contend that it is important to study its relationship with ICTs because they are dependent on each other.

If the impact of advertising could be discerned from the role that Bernstein (1972) ascribed to it, it could be instructive and could provide ammunition for those on the opposite side of the debate on advertising and socioeconomic development. He argued that advertising could be used to exert pressure at the most appropriate time. As a form of persuasive communication, Bernstein (1972) stated:

You can do things in advertisements you can't do elsewhere. You can tell your story the way you want it told. You can include as much information as you want. You can talk to roughly the sort of people you think will be interested. You can exert pressure. . . . You can inject news-value into your product. . . . You can control the image you wish to project. (p. 22)

Considering these factors, McCarty (1994) contended that advertising serves as an important source of information about culture. Taylor, Hoy, and Grubbs (1996) described advertising as a form of cultural communication that expresses a culture's history, values, norms, and beliefs. In most societies, cultural values are viewed as a pervasive medium that governs, organizes, rules, and guides the attitudes, relationships, norms, and existence of people. If advertising is viewed as a conduit of a society's cultural values, McCarty (1994) and Cheng (1997) concurred with Richard Pollay and Katherine Gallagher, who asserted that:

The mirror is distorted . . . because advertising reflects only certain attitudes, behaviors and values. It models and reinforces only certain lifestyles and philosophies, those that serve the seller's interests. It displays those values that are most readily linked to the available products, that are easily dramatized in advertisements, and that are most reliably responded to by consumers who see the advertisements. Advertising is, therefore, a selective reinforcement of only some behaviors and values. (cited in Cheng, 1997, p. 774)

In *Advertising in Contemporary Society*, Kim Rotzoll and James Haefner stated that "advertising (as an institution) must be considered in light of the cultural expectations set for it and that advertising plays different roles in different societies" (cited in Taylor, Hoy, & Grubbs, 1996, pp. 3–4). These scholars view an advertising text as a complex place of articulation, exhibition, and expression between social and political sign systems. Bertelsen (1996) referred to Robert Goldman, whose book, *Reading Ads Socially*, described advertising as that "prime instance of the logic of the commodity form which impacts both materially and ideologically, reifying, and mystifying social logic, framing meanings and organizing the ways we see the world" (Bertelsen, 1996, p. 226).

A wealth of cross-cultural studies have used print and broadcasting advertising to examine the similarities and differences among advertising content, the types of appeals, and the strategies used in one country to those of another. These studies are aimed at helping to raise the understanding of cultural differences to assist international firms to produce effective advertising messages (Lin, 2001; Stafford, 2005; Zandpour et al. 1994). Zandpour et al. (1994) says that these studies establish that differences exist in ad content, appeals, and strategies. These differences are often assumed to reflect the cultural variations of a society. The findings of these and other cross-cultural studies on advertising could arguably be summarized to establish that:

- Most of the studies deal with the interplay between advertising and cultural values within as well as across cultures.
- Most cultural studies on advertising find that advertising in developing nations tends to promote Western values such as high technology, consumerism, and modernism at the expense of the socioeconomic and cultural realities of emerging societies.
- Most of these studies focus on dissimilar cultures; few have examined similar cultures. African countries have been neglected. Cultural values prevailing in a society influence the ad content, appeals, and strategies used in a country. Advertisers also employ universal appeals.
- Some of the cross-cultural advertising studies are based on the debate over standardization and/or globalization of advertising. They produce contrasting results as to their negative or positive benefits and impact.
- Some of the studies have found that advertising contributes to economic growth and press freedom in less developed parts of the world.
- They have largely been drawn and produced from mechanistic and quantitative methods, such as content analysis, at the expense of qualitative methods.

To understand the cultural messages conveyed by advertising, it is necessary to explain divergent interpretations of culture. Parekh (1997) states that if defined broadly, *culture* "refers to the body of beliefs and practices governing the conduct of the relevant area, be it a specific activity, an aspect of human experience, an organization or human life was whole," but when used in an unqualified way, "it may refer to beliefs and practices regulating all or major areas of human life, and have broadly the same meaning as the older term 'a way of life' " (p. 165).

However, when culture is used as an adjective and qualified, Parekh (1997) states that: "the adjective expresses a judgment on it, or points to its bearer, or highlights a specific area of life" (p. 165). Offering an example, Parekh goes on to explain that the term *primitive* is used to describe a way of life judged to be backward and insufficiently advanced, whereas *advanced culture* has the contrary meaning. In contrast, moral or political culture is conceived to be a set of beliefs and practices that govern the conduct of moral and political life, respectively.

Referring to the cultural values and meaning conveyed in advertising, Dyer (1982) states:

> The meaning of an advertisement is not something there, statistically inside an ad, waiting to be revealed by a "correct" interpretation. What

an ad means depends on how it operates, how signs and its "ideological" effect are organized *internally* (within the text) and *externally* (in relation to its production, circulation and consumption and in relation to technological, economic, legal and social relation). . . . Ads are not invisible conveyors of messages or transparent reflections of reality, they are specific discourses or structures of signs. (p. 115)

As a form of mass media artifact, Hyun (1990) states that an advertising text is culturally contextualized (cultural-based principles of meaning) (i.e., its meaning is based on a consumer's interpretation or perception when it is decoded). Advertisers tend to develop (encode) their messages by adapting the cultural values, languages, ideas, and norms shared by a group. Although advertisers and consumers in a society may share common values and meanings, their goals vary: Advertisers use the medium to manipulate and persuade consumers to purchase, whereas consumers use it as a source of information about goods and services that help them make informed purchasing decisions. This process allows advertisers and consumers to participate in the creation, production, and consumption of advertising (Leiss, Kline, & Jhally, 1990). The degree of influence exerted by the advertiser and consumer remains a subject of debate. However, if one considers the purpose of advertising, it could be argued that those who create advertising exert a greater influence because they control the content.

In the West, it may be true that advertisers and consumers share common culturally derived meaning, but this is questionable in developing countries, where the cultural values of dominant Western advertisers (multinationals) and consumers differ. This may account for criticism of the dominance of Western multinational advertising activities in developing nations, where they have been accused of using Western values and promotional appeals to promote consumerism at the expense of socioeconomic development and traditional culture (Fejes, 1980; Janus, 1986).

As explained previously, in both developing and developed parts of the world, the differing goals of advertisers and consumers influence the consumer's interpretation of advertising messages. A consumer's understanding of a message in an advertisement occurs consciously or unconsciously and is influenced by a group's socially shared values, but not necessarily by individual traits (S. Hall, 1980). However, it should be noted that the meaning consumers ascribe to advertising might not be the intended message an advertiser planned to convey. The conflict between the goal of advertisers and consumers' interpretation of advertising messages may account for the controversy regarding the role that advertising plays in most societies.

This debate has contributed to the growing use of qualitative approaches such as the critical-cultural approach to explore the cultural values conveyed in advertising artifacts to determine their meaning.

Critical analysts rely on artifacts used or produced in a particular culture for analysis. Concerned with the generation of meaning, cultural analysis is essentially Marxist in the traditions of Louis Althusser and Antonio Gramsci, although the approach is inflected with structuralist and ethnographic accents (Fiske, 1992).

RESEARCH METHODS AND APPLICATIONS

Thus, this chapter uses qualitative content analysis (a combination of quantitative and qualitative approaches) to answer the following research questions:

- What are the dominant positive cultural values and ideas found in Nigerian advertisements?
- What are the dominant negative values and ideas found in Nigerian advertisements?
- What are the positive values and ideas absent in these advertisements?
- What are the negative values and ideas absent in these advertisements?
- Are universal values conveyed in Nigerian mass media advertisements?

Qualitative content analysis utilizes techniques that identify and explain patterns within a collection of texts (Berg, 2001). Qualitative content analysis allows a scholar to explore the cultural, ideological mindset, themes, topics, and symbols revealed in an artifact such as advertising (Berg, 2001). Alaniz and Wilkes (1995) state that in recent years scholars have begun to show their impatience with the mere counting of symbolic objects, an approach typically employed in content analysis. Instead, scholars have turned their attention to critical analysis to study advertising texts holistically, instead of counting numbers. The change, they explained, was due to the fact that the traditional social science approaches were reductionist in nature. Critical analysis examines the underlying meaning of advertisements within the context of the cultural world for which they were produced and received.

Quantitative content analysis is defined as a systematic collection and objective interpretation of communication with the goal of determining the manifest of an advertising content and quantifying them (Kerlinger, 1986). However, quantitative content analysis is not the focus of this chapter. It is not used for interpreting and measuring data. Content analysis is only used for the systematic selection of advertisements to be analyzed to overcome the criticism that studies using qualitative approaches rely on a small number of artifacts not chosen systematically (Wimmer & Dominick, 1994). It should be noted that this is a baseline study, thus no a priori content categories were used. Data on the position, size, and frequency were not gathered. Rather, this study relies on a qualitative approach to explore the discourse conveyed in the selected advertisements. Qualitative analysis does not call for measuring intercoder reliability or determining validity.

POPULATION OF THE STUDY AND DATA COLLECTION

This study uses content analysis to systematically select 500-plus advertisements published in Nigerian print media in the 1998 and those aired on broadcast media in 1998 and 1999. This is to have a universal set of advertisements from Nigerian mass media. Only TV advertisements were obtained from a convenient sample of advertisements available and aired at Lagos State Television during the last quarter of 1998 and the first quarter of 1999. Logistical problems dealing with power failures made it difficult to obtain a systematic sample of TV advertisements. The TV station, owned by Lagos State Broadcasting Corporation, provided 22 (4 percent) of the advertisements analyzed.

The sample of radio advertisements was taped from three commercial radio stations in Lagos, Nigeria. The taping took place simultaneously. Advertisements from radio were taped over a 2-week period from January 25 through February 8, 1999, between 7–9 a.m. and 6–10 p.m. Radio advertisements came from three commercial stations. The commercial radio stations are Rhythm Rhythm FM 93.7, Ray Power 100.5 FM, and Cool FM 96.9. They provided 57 (10 percent) of the sample. Based on listener surveys, these radio stations are regarded as the most popular in Lagos and other parts of the country where they can be heard. Nigeria does not have a systematic rating system like Nielsen. These radio and TV stations are based in Lagos, Nigeria's commercial capital. Broadcast advertisements accounted for 79 (14 percent) of the sample of the advertisements in this study.

Three of Nigeria's leading newspapers, *The Guardian*, *ThisDay*, and *Daily Times*, provided 434 (77 percent) of the sample of 566. The newspaper sample was drawn from three of Nigeria's leading newspapers in a 14-day sample period. Dates included in the study were obtained by creating a composite 2-week period for each newspaper during the last quarter of 1998 (Wimmer & Dominick, 1994). A sample representing each week day was selected at random. For example, a sample of two Monday issues for *The Guardian* was randomly selected from the 12 possible Mondays during the period, followed by each day of the week until every day of the week was represented twice for each newspaper.

All display advertisements appearing in every weekly issue of *Tell* and *Newswatch*, published during the last quarter of 1998, were included. The period produced 12 issues for each magazine for a total of 24. Eleven issues of *Tell* and 12 issues of *Newswatch* were included in the sample. One issue of *Tell* was not found. Twenty-three magazine issues were analyzed.

Two Nigerian weekly magazines, *Tell* and *Newswatch* both privately owned, provided 53 (9 percent) of the sample analyzed. As the largest circulating newspapers and magazines, advertisements appearing in these print outlets enjoy the greatest amount of exposure among Nigerian readers. Although this study incorporates radio and TV, the bulk of the analysis dealt with print advertisements because they reach a national audience. It should be noted that radio is the most common form of communication in Nigeria, but most radio advertisements are usually regional in nature, rely on regional dialects, and reach a regional audience.

Duplicate advertisements were eliminated, and noncommercial advertisements such as obituaries and advertorials (ads containing editorial as well as promotional messages) were not included.

APPROACHES TO CULTURAL CRITICAL AND TEXTUAL ANALYSES

The intentional or unintentional ability of mass media artifacts such as advertising to produce, represent, and emphasize some forms of images and realities of the world is what a British sociologist calls "politics of signification" (S. Hall, 1977). With this phrase, Hall contends that the messages conveyed and the artifacts represented in mass media promote the interests as well as the values of the elites who control the means of production.

However, Vande Berg, Wenner, and Gronbeck (1998) and Brummett (1994) state that cultural theorists attempt to formulate ways in which mass media artifacts can be used to resist the ideas and products of the dominant class. To address the debate and interpret an advertisement, Brummett states that a critical study assumes three characteristics, becming:

1. critical in attitude and method;
2. concerned with power; and
3. Interventionist.

The first characteristic of cultural analysis is that it is critical in attitude and method. This means a critical analyst adopts an attitude of suspicion by assuming things are often other than (or more than) they seem (counterintuitive explanations). This attitude is not intended to be negative, hostile, or destructive. However, it helps to ascertain what else may be occurring in addition to the obvious by adopting an interrogative approach that answers questions about meaning, complexity, and evaluation.

The second characteristic of critical study relates to its concern with power. Referring to this characteristic, Brummett (1994) observes, "critical studies examine what power is or what it has been understood to be, and how power is created, maintained, shared, lost, and seized" (p. 76). He adds that, "critical studies assume that most of the time, people experience power in ways that are similar to the experiences of other members of their groups" (p. 76). If so, one could argue that, during this era of globalization, multinational corporations advertising from capitalistic societies will continue to strive to maintain their dominance in the developing world as technological development shrinks the world, thus promoting stiffer economic competition.

The third characteristic of a critical study concerns its interventionist nature. As an outgrowth of its critical attitude and method, the concern for power allows a critical analyst to get involved in the issue being investigated to create change. For example, it has been argued that multinational corporations promote the value of consumption in developing nations, degrade the environment, and neglect the welfare of its workers.

The hidden values embedded in an advertisement can be brought to the forefront by critical analysis (Stern, 1988). The concept of preferred reading was developed to explain how mass media artifacts could be examined critically (Hall, 1980). The theory has three strategies: dominant reading, negotiated reading, and oppositional reading. Those who agree with the messages presented in mass media produce dominant reading, whereas those who fit into the dominant ideology, but have not established a firm position, produce negotiated reading. Those who disagree with the messages conveyed by the mass media produce oppositional reading.

It has been argued that any analysis of mass media artifacts must attempt to answer the following questions (Griffin, 1995; Vande Berg, Wenner, & Gronbeck, 1998): What institutions and symbols are used to maintain the power, interests, and means of production for the sake of the elites and preservation of the dominant ideology? What are the cultural and ideological conflicts, issues, and perspectives conveyed in the artifact? What are the entrenched societal values manifested in the advertisements?

To answer these questions, cultural theorists and analysts rely on their personal experiences and views to interpret and uncover the dominant values and contexts conveyed in an advertisement. It is important to note that two scholars may provide different interpretations of an advertising message. This could be attributed to the fact that an advertisement carries more than one message (Pajnik & Lesjak-Tusek, 2002).

Relying on Brummet's (1994) critical technique and Frith's (1997) three-stage approach, the following in-depth critical and detailed analysis of a Cadbury advertisement serves as an example to explain how each of the 500-plus advertisements were analyzed to discern the dominant values and contexts they convey, as presented on Table 7.2. The author provides a detailed analysis of a Cadbury's advertisement because it is produced by the subsidiary of a multinational company. Cadbury's advertisements are common in radio, TV, and print, and they reach a large segment of Nigeria. Nigerians recall this specific advertisement and others created by Cadbury and exposed in the Nigerian mass media. Thus, the author assumes this advertisement has some degree of influence and conveys dominant values and contexts common in Nigerian mass media advertisements as presented in Table 2.

APPLICATION OF ANALYTICAL APPROACH

The first stage of the analysis involves exploring the surface meaning of the advertisements by recording every object on the advertisement in the analysis sheet without offering any interpretation. The second stage involves a closer reading and identifying the advertiser's intended meaning by exploring discursive strategies conveyed in the advertisements. Symbols, themes, values, headlines, narrative structure, meanings, tone, and omissions are recorded on the analysis sheets. This process allows the analyst to explore the hidden implications of the advertisement and to determine themes that may be missing. The final stage involves discerning the cultural and/or ideological meaning. To discern the subjective or cultural forms in the texts, the analysis sheets are used as a guide to explore the recurrent patterns and dominant themes, as well as the missing values to offer interpretation of the findings within the framework of critical analysis.

The detailed analysis of Cadbury's advertisement, followed by a brief analysis of some of the 500-plus advertisements in this study, demonstrates how the author obtained the dominant values (positive or negative) outlined in Table 7.2. The process was used to discern the missing values. A dominant value(s) is described as the most obvious value within the context or message the author assumes an advertisement conveys. This study defines a positive value as one that reflects Nigerian and African cultural traditional social values (Moemeka, 1997; Obeng-Quaidoo, 1986) and conveys virtues of advertising (Langrehr & Caywood, 1989) or universal cultural values (Murdock, 1955) outlined. These include savings, family, national unity and integration, good health, communitarianism, respect for nature and authority, hard work, wisdom, and temperance.

In contrast, values classified as negative include Western-oriented values such as sex, youth, exploitation of nature, image, and individualism, values not reflected among Nigerian and African traditional core values (Moemeka, 1997; Obeng-Quaidoo, 1986). A value is also described as having a negative connotation if it conveys the seven cardinal sins, including greed, lust, sloth, pride, anger, gluttony, and anger (Langrehr & Caywood, 1989). A value is defined as missing if it is not found in the advertisements analyzed. The analysis also used the following table of valuse the Malaysian government has suggested cultural assist or hinder in the process of

Table 7.1   Malaysian Values (Dualistic Pairs of Competitive Concepts)

National Interest .... Ethnic Interest
Moderation .... Extremism
Tolerance .... Intolerance
Mutual Respect .... Prejudice
National Pride/Loyalty .... Loyalty to Other Nations
Hardwork .... Idleness
Perseverance .... Defeatism
Discipline .... Disorderliness
Delayed Gratification .... Instant Gratification
Enterprising .... Nonactivity
Cooperation .... Self-Sufficiency
Excellence .... Mediocrity
Environmental Degradation .... Environmental Protection
Respect (Deference .... Impertinence/Discourteous/Curt
Indirection .... Bluntness
Dissimulation .... Brutal Honesty
Ordered/Self-Control .... Unruly
Ethical/Moral .... Unethical
Kindness/Good Deed .... Selfish/Inconsiderate
Patience .... Impatience/Rashness
Acceptance .... Complaining
Sincerity .... Ulterior Motive

Scheme Based:
Clifford Geertz. 1960. *The Religion of Java.* Chicago: The University of Chicago Press.
Shaharuddin Maaruf. 1984. *Concept a Hero in Malay Society. The Midterm Review of the Fourth Malaysian Plan. 1984.*
Adopted from Darinah Ahmad. 1995. *Cultural Imperialism Through Advertising: The Case of Advertising in Malaysia.* p. 90.

modernization to classify the message conveyed in advertisements under analysis. Those values are presented on Table 7.1.

CADBURY ADVERTISEMENT: AN EXEMPLAR

The Surface Meaning

This advertisement, on the back page of the issue, is a graphic collage portraying nine people representing different professional and working backgrounds. The professionals portrayed include a physician, a nurse, a businessman, a scientist, and two athletes (a football player and a tennis player). All are dressed in their professional outfits and seem ready to begin work. The only nonprofessional is a factory worker, who is wearing traditional attire and a hat. The football player is wearing a jersey and is poised to kick a ball, while the tennis player is wearing blue shorts and a white shirt. He seems to be engaged in a game. Of the nine, three are women. One of the three women is a scientist. She is wearing a lab gown bearing Cadbury's logo, indicating that she works for the company. The photos are placed to the left and right sides of the copy. The text is placed in the center beneath a blaring headline that reads:

WE SEE THE FUTURE (Newswatch, 1998, Nov. 16, back cover)

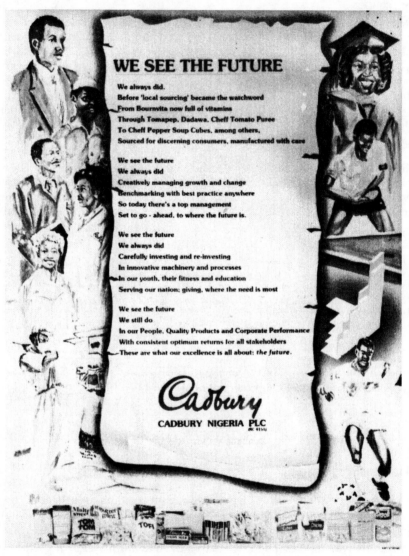

Figure 7.1   Cadury, *Newswatch*, 1998, Nov. 16, printed with permission of *Newswatch*, Lagos, Cadbury Nigeria PLC., Lagos.

The headline's type size is estimated to be about 17 points, whereas the text is about 12 points. The name of the company is displayed at the end of the text. Cadbury's name is typed in purple and italicized for added distinction. The various beverages that Cadbury produces are displayed from the right to left sides at the bottom of the page. On the right side, the advertisement displays a staircase along graphics of some of the professionals. Present on the top stair is the symbol for Nigerian currency [naira] and the letter "M" behind the symbol. The "M" represents million. The attractiveness of this advertisement is enhanced by the use of color. Few advertisements use color in Nigeria.

The Advertiser's Intended Meaning

The aim of portraying people in different professions underscores the fact that Cadbury has fed and continues to provide nutritious food to these people to make them healthy and energetic as they look to the future as the headline implies. The advertisement also promotes the value of family and collectiveness by grouping people (Nigerians) of various professions together. The staircase demonstrates that those who use Cadbury climb the ladder of success as its slogan states: "Pursuit of excellence."

The Cultural or Ideological Meaning

This advertisement appears on the back cover of *Newswatch*, one of Nigeria's leading magazines, read by Nigerian elites. By displaying the professionals and its products on the back cover of a leading magazine, Cadbury is telling the citizens that successful people have relied and still rely on its products for food and good health. To be successful, the advertisement implies that you must use Cadbury's products as part of your diet. It tells the public that only successful individuals can afford its products.

The women the advertisement portrays have prominent roles: a nurse, a college graduate, and a scientist. The scientist works for Cadbury. The advertisement conveys the message that women are playing important roles in society, and Cadbury is at the forefront of employing and recognizing women for their contribution to the workforce. This is not true. Women have made gains in Nigeria, but they remain subordinate to men. However, because Nigerian women are responsible for the bulk of household purchases, Cadbury realizes it must appeal to women to maintain or increase sales.

It should be noted that Cadbury has been operating in Nigeria for decades. It remains one of the most profitable Nigerian companies. Yet the company is not known for offering scholarships to students or promoting research in Nigerian universities for agricultural development and food production. It is vaguely regarded as a sponsor for health programs that educate people. Cadbury does not participate in efforts to feed the poor. The failure of Cadbury and other multinationals to invest in Nigeria prompts one to question how Nigeria will build a prosperous future. The advertisement fails to mention that the Nigerian masses cannot afford this product—its products remain in the province of the elite. Although the purpose of advertising is to compel a consumer to purchase a product, critics allege that such exposure promotes engagement in illegal activities to acquire money to purchase unaffordable goods and services and discourages saving.

Based on this analysis, one could argue that this advertisement conveys several values. It promotes positive values such as hard work, success, and equality of women and good health. However, while portraying women in professional roles, the advertisement told them they must perform their role of feeding the family if they are to be healthy and strive for success. This message puts women in their place as homemakers and subordinates to their husbands. The advertisement does not portray men carrying out household activities. Although Africans view motherhood as a virtue in Africa, Cadbury sends contradictory messages. The advertisement promotes women as professionals and should not remind the public of their subordinate role at home when it did not do so for men.

BRIEF DECONSTRUCTION OF 500-PLUS ADVERTISEMENTS

Family as a Conveyor of Values

A hallmark of human existence is the ability to procreate. To bring another human being into the world is to assume the responsibility of caring and loving for that person. In Africa, an individual's love and care do not cease at the nuclear family level. The responsibility reaches to the extended family, the community, the workplace, and society. This may account for the use of family and communal human relationships as the key means of conveying other values in Nigerian advertisements.

Advertisements in Nigerian mass media tend to use family to convey other values such as togetherness (*Tell*, Oct. 5, 1998:18), caring fatherhood, respect, authority (*ThisDay*, 1998), and hard work, which could be considered universal values because they are not in African and various other cultures. For example, in its radio spots, Cadbury Nigeria (Plc.), the maker of Bournvita, reminds parents that they must take care of their children by feeding them its product. The advertisement states that every child deserves nourishment for his or her well-being, and those who consume Bournvita will develop into healthy children. The advertiser realizes the emphasis the Nigerian value system places on family.

Good Health

Cadbury is one of many food manufacturers that claim their products provide good health for the family. In their radio spots, the producers of Sonola cooking oil, Lipton tea, Lipton super seasoning, and NASCO biscuits and corn flakes promote their products as tasteful and healthful. The radio advertisement for Lipton's super seasoning urges Nigerians to use the condiment to "wake up the flavor of your meals." The spot for Lipton's tea advises Nigerians that the company's tea is what families need to start and end the day in an active manner.

NASCO claims that its products provide vital minerals and rapidly stop hunger. The producer of Orheptal blood tonic also uses family appeal to promote the product. In a radio spot, families are reminded that the product is also available in capsule form. The spot claims that Orheptal blood tonic purifies the blood, revitalizes a person, and rejuvenates the body after a day of hard work. The advertisement implies that a healthy and vital family is a proud one and demonstrates that the family serves as a larger entity where all members take care of each other.

Security

Cornerstone Insurance (Plc.) uses the portrait of a sad-looking mother and her children (a boy and girl) to implore the public (heads of families) to take out life insurance policies and invest for the future security of the family. The advertisement implies that this is essential for the family's financial well-being in case the breadwinner can no longer provide for the family as a result of job loss or death. The message implies that failure to do so creates "pains that time alone cannot heal" (*ThisDay*, 1998, p. 24). If the breadwinner fails to purchase a policy, the head of household does not provide financial security for the family.

Protection

Using protection as a theme in radio, Johnson Wax, producer of Raid Aerial insect killer, urges Nigerians to protect their families from diseases such as malaria by spraying with the insecticide before bedtime to kill mosquitoes. The advertisement describes the insecticide as people-friendly because the product does not cause colds or coughs generally associated with other insecticides. The advertisement claims that the insecticide is "gentle on you and deadly on insects." The producer of Red Pentex toothpaste claims its product cleans a person's teeth and refreshes the breath.

Motherhood

Family is also used in two TV advertisements to promote a detergent and cooking oil. Both TV spots show a mother in a home environment using one of these products. In the detergent advertisement, two large bowls containing laundry are shown as a mother uses her hands to wash the clothes. The water in one of the bowls (containing the dirty clothes) looks dirty, whereas the other bowl (containing the washed clothes) looks bright. In a Sonola cooking oil TV advertisement, a wide shot of a mother is shown using Sonola cooking oil to prepare her family's meal. The mother implies in her statement that the cooking oil enables her to prepare tasteful and nutritious food for the family. These advertisements use motherhood as an appeal to show that Nigerian mothers care for their families. The detergent advertisement demonstrates that by washing the family's clothing the mother is keeping her household clean and free from germs that might cause illness. The cooking oil advertisement demonstrates that mothers keep their families healthy and strong by providing the household with tasteful and nutritious food.

Fatherhood and Respect for Authority

One of Bic's advertisements demonstrates the role of the family. The advertisement also uses family to convey other values. In the advertisement, a father dressed in business attire stands on the side and watches his son as the child does his homework. The text of the advertisement reads, "Writing well is a tradition that runs in the family" (*ThisDay*, 1998, p. 8). The advertisement portrays the father as a successful man. The advertisement implies a man who commands authority and respect and must be emulated by his children and others in the community. The message was designed to encourage people to learn from this successful father who used Bic pens during his climb to the top.

Collectivism

Studies show that more than 1 million Nigerians suffer from diabetes, which might lead to stroke, heart attack, kidney disease, impaired vision, and sudden death. Armed with these statistics, Neithmeth International Pharmaceuticals (Plc.) places an advertisement to remind Nigerians of the need for regular physicals. The advertisement shows a healthy-looking son talking to his pot-bellied father. The message urges Nigerians to show "this page to your family and friends" because "you could save a life" (*Tell*, 1998, p. 18). This promotion tends to promote the concept of collectivism (Hofstede, 1980, 1983).

National Unity

To promote human relationships and development at societal levels, Mutual Life and General Insurance Limited describes itself as a firm that cares, shares, and unites forever its predominantly Nigerian customers. Using the picture of two birds clinging together to signify unity, the copy reads: "To Care, and Share, Together Forever" remains its corporate goal (*The Guardian*, 1998, p. 64). The theme of unity is important in a nation where ethnic and cultural differences pull citizens apart.

Gift Giving

As a reader flips through the pages of a Nigerian newspaper, he or she may learn that gift giving remains the mode of showing loyalty, generosity, care, and appreciation—at the family, communal, and societal levels. Advertisements promoting goods for gifts that can be offered to families, colleagues, individuals, corporate employees, and employers are plentiful in Nigerian mass media. In an advertisement showing the pictures of assorted forms of gifts, Signature states: "A gift should bring more than just momentary pleasure. It should last for more than a day. And it should remind the recipient of you for years to come" (*ThisDay*, 1998). During the Christmas season, Hennessy uses seasonal ornaments to remind people that it is a period for gift giving (*ThisDay*, 1998, p. 32). The implication of this advertisement is that, as one celebrates, one should not forget friends and relatives.

Savings

Savings is a dominant theme found in this study of Nigerian mass media advertisements. Saving is encouraged through the promotion of sales and discounts. In one advertisement, AKAI electronics tells its customers they will derive real value for their money, as well as enjoy a great picture and sound if they buy their TV sets at low prices (*ThisDay*, 1998). A French Airline (*The Guardian*, 1998) urges Nigerians traveling abroad to use its Airbus A310 to get to any European destination at the low fare of $310 (one way) and $620 (round trip). The normal price could be more than $1,000. This promotion, which encourages Nigerians to travel out of the country, does not help Nigeria's economic development because it encourages the depletion of foreign currency reserves in a country where foreign exchange remains scarce.

In its radio advertisement, United Bank for Africa advises Nigerians they will be as wise as their ancestors if they choose to deposit their money with the bank. The message implies that savings encourages thrift. United Bank is not the only Nigerian bank that encourages savings. Most banking advertisements convey the same message. For example, in addition to promoting many of its services, Triumph Merchant Bank (Plc.) urges Nigerians to save with the bank (*The Guardian*, 1998). However, it should be noted that some savings programs promoted by banks are out of reach for most Nigerians. Some savings programs require thousands to a million naira (Nigerian currency). For example, Triumph's Gold Shield Account promotes a savings program that requires a minimum deposit of 1 million naira. Most Nigerians cannot afford to invest such huge sums.

Respect and Exploitation of Nature

Recognizing that African cultures relate to and celebrate nature, Vita-biotics, a pharmaceutical company, reminded Nigerians as they cele-brated 38 years of nationhood to "pray all of our dreams and visions be accomplished in a world where nature meets science" (*The Guardian*, 1998, p. 10).

In one advertisement, the National Inland Waterways uses the pic-ture of a duck floating on a river to demonstrate its commitment to nature. The advertisement implies that the agency views nature as a gift that should not be damaged. Another of its advertisement reads: "We've taken to change like a duck to water" (*ThisDay*, 1998, p. 20). The agency states its commitment to promote water transportation by regulating navigation, in addition to ensuring the development of facili-ties and inland waterway networks. Promoting harmony with nature, another advertisement by the agency uses a picture showing a group of people using a traditional wooden canoe powered by a small engine on a waterway near a big city skyline to encourage people to take a voyage (*Newswatch*, 1998).

By failing to use a paddleboat, this advertisement fails at its goal of promoting the natural use of Nigeria's waterways. However, another advertisement in this series demonstrates that using only paddle canoes may not accommodate the number of people who need transportation. In this advertisement, people are seen milling around a river platform on a riverbank to board a passenger boat. National Inland Waterways reit-erates its goal of simplifying everyday life by tapping into the resources of water, which is also the source of life (*Newswatch* 1998).

In a radio advertisement, the maker of Sonola cooking oil also recog-nizes the importance that Africans place in nature by touting Sonala as a natural product made from bean seeds. The advertisement describes Sonola as the natural choice with a *paapaa taeste*. *Paapaa taeste* is Pidgin English that represents "choice taste."

National Service and Socioeconomic Development

Service is another value that Nigerian advertisers promote. For example, when Universal Trust Bank promotes its service to help individuals and businesses pay their Value Added Tax (VAT) and other tax obligations, the advertisement takes a patriotic tone. The headline reads, "It pays to pay your VAT and other taxes" through Universal Trust (*ThisDay*,

1998, p. 9). The bank assures every customer of "prompt, efficient and courteous service" (*ThisDay*, 1998, p. 8). Conveying that the bank appreciates its customers, the advertisement reminds Nigerians that the payment of taxes is "a very special feeling, at fulfilling a national obligation" (*ThisDay*, 1998, p. 8).

Spiritual Well-Being

In a radio spot, Pentecostal Fellowship of Nigeria says it will present leading Nigerian religious clergymen at a revival themed "End-Time Revival." The advertisement invites Nigerians to attend, be anointed, and become spiritually revived for the "End-Time." The radio spot implies that attending the revival will help the attendees to renew themselves as they deal with life's mundane concerns. A Christian bookstore uses a similar appeal. In a radio spot, the bookstore urges Nigerians to purchase religious books, cassettes, and videos for use at their convenience. The spot describes these religious-related materials as a great "source of life."

Youth and Image

Youth and image dominate cigarette advertisements in Nigeria. This is evident in TV as well as magazine advertisements. Transnational companies like Philip Morris and Rothmans sponsor these advertisements. The TV commercials predominantly feature white and or Western models, whereas the print advertisements include non-white, Western, and African models. They are often filmed in the West and in urban settings. The messages promoted by these cigarette commercials convey the idea that smoking is a fashionable trend. They advocate cigarette smoking as a youthful activity that builds friendship among cohorts. Also, the messages imply that smoking is a sign of success and promotes good health. These messages are in sharp contrast to studies that prove cigarette smoking causes diseases that could lead a young person to an untimely death.

According to a report on National Public Radio's news program "Weekend All Things Considered," a study by the World Health Organization found that smoking would be the single leading cause of death worldwide in the next 30 years (National Public Radio, 1999). In many Western countries, cigarette advertising is restricted. To find new markets, cigarette companies advertise aggressively in developing nations where regulation remains lax (*The Indian Express*, *The Financial Times*, and Reuters, 1997). It should be noted that cigarette promotions in Nigerian mass media often include a government warning that smokers are likely to die young.

Table 7.2   Dominant Cultural Values Present in Nigerian Mass Media Advertising

Dominant Positive Cultural Values

•	•	•	•	•	•
Family	Love	Savings	Gift Giving	Endurance	Security
•	•	•	•	•	•
Collectivism	Mother-hood	Protection	Truth	Honesty	Wisdom
•	•	•	•	•	•
Ambition	Service	Nature	Care	Good Health	Pidgin English

• Togetherness   • Technology
• Personal Development   • Spiritual Development

Dominant Negative Cultural Values

•	•	•	•		•
Consumerism	Pleasure	Youth	Image		Sex
•	•	•	•		•
Dependence	Corruption	Laziness	Foreign / Western Symbols		Consumerism

• Economic Distortion

EXPLORATION OF NEGATIVE AND MISSING CULTURAL VALUES

The Negative Implications

Discerning the critical discourse used in these advertisements and the ways that meanings are denoted in their messages is the main goal of this study. It should be noted that the advertisements analyzed connote additional meanings than those that have been identified, and the interpretation of meanings in the advertisements should be considered subjective depending on the analyst's philosophy and theoretical approach (Pajnik & Lesjak-Tusek, 2002). In contrast, a person's interpretation can always be followed by what could be called a "circle of meaning" (Derrida, 1981; cited in Pajnik & Lesjak-Tusek, 2002). The meanings are constantly produced and reproduced depending on the cultural contexts and the specific time and place.

Based on this exploration, the author believes that some of the cultural values used for promotion, such as youth, beauty, pleasure, and consumerism, could be considered negative as well as Western-oriented. For example, technological products like cars, stereos, and air conditioners are used to promote pleasure. It could be said that the promotion of consumerism and pleasure with products that most Nigerians cannot afford could frustrate the masses. It also could inhibit and distort the development of the economy. The inability of the masses to acquire these expensive products may breed jealousy of the elites by the masses.

On the part of the elites, the drive to acquire these consumer goods to maintain their lifestyles may prompt them to disregard their societal and work responsibilities. The resulting effect of such promotion may be corruption. It may contribute to the neglect of the masses by the elites. For example, it has been alleged that Nigerian officials retain two or more jobs and other interests to earn enough money to maintain their standard of living. It has also been alleged that Nigerian payrolls contain an untold number of ghost workers (Ollor-Obari, 1999). The money wasted to pay these ghost workers could be used to contribute to the employment and welfare of the living.

Nigerian mass media advertisements implore parents to take care of their children. The reliance of children on their parents may inhibit the ability of the youth to independently work for economic and social mobility. However, the reliance on family (communalism) encourages people to cater to the welfare of family members. As a result, individual aspirations and achievements may be inhibited.

Because most Africans defer to the wisdom of older people, it may inhibit the youth from taking initiative on their own. It also may produce excessive fear of authority. For example, the producer of ProCold demonstrates this phenomenon in a radio spot when a boss who suffers from a cold leaves his office to seek relief. While out, he takes ProCold, which "healed" him quickly. On his return, he finds one of his subordinates in his office. Without allowing the subordinate to explain what he is doing, the boss accuses him of "turning my office into a hotel." The boss becomes angry and admonishes his subordinate. The subordinate begins to weep, instead of explaining what he is doing in the office. He continues weeping as the boss tells that him he is suspended for 2 weeks. This suspension could be without pay. In contrast, the subordinate might have been weeping out of a sense of guilt and was trying to get the older person to relent by evoking sympathy. African tradition calls on an older person, or a person in a position of authority, to adopt a course of action that will not cause undue hardship on a subordinate.

As stated earlier, most of the models appearing in Nigerian advertisements use young people and tend to promote youth and image (*ThisDay*, 1998). Some companies also use image to promote their products without explaining the benefits of the products. For example, in one radio spot, the bottling company that produces Krest claims that taking Krest distinguishes the user from the masses. However, the bottlers of Sprite, a rival soft drink, seem to chide Krest for relying on image as an appeal. In a radio spot, Sprite claims that it is not concerned with image, but is concerned with helping people to quench their thirst.

Broadcast and print cigarette advertisements use young models to promote Western consumerism. The use of youth and image undermines the deference given to old age. The producer of Gulder beer in a radio spot urges Nigerians to indulge in its product because it enhances life. Such advertisements promote consumerism and mislead Nigerians because they claim that alcohol creates fun and promotes good health. Numerous studies demonstrate that alcohol causes ill health and brings misery and death to people as a result of untimely deaths associated with drunk driving (*Post Express Wired*, 1998).

In several radio spots, the proprietors of restaurants promote eating at their trendy restaurants and cafes where expensive items such as ice cream, beverages, and fast-food products are sold. These spots are promoted in a country where families continue to struggle daily for adequate meals.

In its radio advertisement, the producer of Moukafoam seems to promote laziness. In this advertisement, a wife attempts to wake up her husband to prepare for work; however, the husband is recalcitrant and tells his wife to permit him to enjoy the comfort of Moukafoam a little longer. He keeps resisting.

Although many service-related advertisements promote harmony with nature, those promoting manufactured and technical products regard nature as a force that must be conquered. It is alleged that Nigerian oil companies are prone to neglect the environment while exploiting the resources. Oil exploration companies and producers of oil-related products such as gas are known to pollute the environment (Korie, 1997).

For more than 25 years, people in the delta region of Nigeria (Nigeria's oil-producing area) have been fighting with Western multinational companies for destroying their environment. For example, the people of Ogoni rely on the bodies of water and lands for their sustenance fishing and farming. Since oil was discovered in the area and Shell began its operations, the land and water in Ogoni land have been polluted and destroyed. Shell has made hundreds of millions of dollars in profit from their exploration in Ogoniland and other oil-producing areas, but they have not contributed to the social development of these areas. Joblessness, poverty, ill health, and illiteracy remain common. In recent years, the Ogonis and other ethnic groups in the delta have been forced to extract compensation and social development from oil companies and the federal government (George & Ogbondah, 1999).

The Missing Values

The core African cultural value system regards religion as a way of life and views the community, instead of the individual, as the paramount value (Moemeka 1997; Obeng-Quaidoo, 1986). It recognizes the sanctity of authority and respect for old age. The system places emphasis on the value of time and its influence and calls for working in harmony with nature. Some of these values are missing. For example, this critical analysis reveals that few individuals of middle age appear in the advertisements, and older individuals are virtually absent. The failure to use Nigeria's older citizens demonstrates that the advertisers do not show the same deference to age that Nigerian tradition requires.

With regard to African religions, none of the advertisements in this analysis refers to African deities or religious celebrations and ways of life. Although some Christian symbols can be found, Nigeria has a large population of Muslims and animists. Islamic and animist symbols are not found.

There are pains that time alone cannot heal

This of course is not an ideal family photograph, but for some who have been forever robbed of a vital family member, this picture for a lifetime remains the new family portrait. Accidents occur when we least expect. But a timely precautionary measure could save us and our loved ones from avoidable anguish.

As you consolidate on the blessings of a year that is gradually winding up, remember, a solid insurance foundation is the cornerstone of a secured future.

CORNERSTONE INSURANCE PLC.

136 Lewis Street, (1st-3rd Floors), Lagos.
P O. Box 75370, Victoria Island, Lagos.
Tel: 2631832, 2636140, 2632863, 2630772, 2637488, 2637393 Fax: 2633079

Photo 7.2   Corner Stone Insurance PLC., *ThisDay*, 1998, Nov. 29, p. 24, printed with permission of *ThisDay*, Lagos and Corner Stone Insurance PLC., Lagos.

Photo 7.3 Universal Trust Bank, *ThisDay*, 1998, Oct. 8, p. 9, printed with permission of *ThisDay*. Lagos, and Universal Trust Bank, Lagos.

Photo 7.4 Tura, USA, *ThisDay*, 1998, Dec. 12, p. 7, printed with permission of *ThisDay*, Lagos and Glemco Industries, Ltd., Lagos.

8 Conclusions and Managerial/ Public Policy Implications

Breakthroughs in ICTs are making the world accessible and international commerce and business more globally interreliant. The trend toward a seamless global economy seems unavoidable (Chen & Starosta, 1998) as governments adopt policies, develop infrastructure, and establish trade blocs to encourage international trade. In this era of expanded international cooperation and trade, advertising serves as an important vehicle to relay information about people, markets, products, and services with the assistance of ICTs. Thus, they are playing, and will continue to play, an important role in international trade and communication.

Considering the increasingly global nature of the world economy and the need to forge closer relations, in the mid-1990s, the Clinton administration called on Congress to pass the African Growth and Opportunity Act, aimed at promoting international trade with sub-Saharan Africa. The passage of the trade act prompted Nelson Mandela, former president of South Africa, to state that he welcomes a trade relationship that treats the continent as an equal and not one that will continue to allow Western nations and corporations to exploit the continent's resources and the labor of the masses. Mandela spoke for many Africans who realize Africa has been failed by Western models of economic development that promote reliance on technological innovations, advertising, and other forms of communication as a tool for social development (Anikulapo, 2001).

In view of these concerns about the place of Africa in the global economy, this study attempts to discern the status of Nigeria and other countries in sub-Saharan Africa regarding the acquisition of technology. It examines the role of advertising in the economic development of Nigeria by exploring the values and symbols conveyed in Nigerian mass media advertisements. A goal of exploring the state of Nigeria's technological development is to suggest the modalities that Nigerian and other governments in sub-Saharan Africa may undertake in their efforts to acquire ICTs. Another aim is to discern whether Nigerian mass media advertisements promote products or expose the social conditions in the country and the role advertising plays in socioeconomic development.

One of the primary research questions examined dealt with the status and role of ICTs in Africa in an increasingly interdependent global economy. The exploration of this subject demonstrates that African nations continue to lag behind other nations of the world in terms of the development of communication facilities (Fortner, 1993). For example, the Information Telecommunication Union (ITU) estimated that Africa's teledensity varied from 0.08 in Chad to .0.46 in Nigeria and other nations in sub-Saharan Africa. This is the case with the other three technologies (electricity, satellite, and computer) driving the global economy in the Information Age.

Like other developing regions (Amin & Gher, 2000), political instability and the lack of economic capability may be blamed for the dismal status of ICTs in Africa. Other factors include dominant government ownership, the technoconnectivity problem, the literacy problem, and the oral culture of Africans. However, answers may be available in the future as African economies and politics stabilizes. Answers also may be found as governments in the region and concerned supranational organizations, such as the United Nations, embark on projects to assist African nations to catch up with other parts of the world in the development of infrastructure for ICTs.

As Nigerian and other governments in sub-Saharan African privatize and liberalize their telecommunications sector to enhance the acquisition of ICTs, they should tread carefully on their paths by adopting a "balanced action" approach. A balanced action constitutes six elements and requires African governments to:

1. avoid foreign loans and spend only a fraction of their annual budgets (within 5 to 10 percent if possible) on acquiring ICTs;
2. liberalize their policies and encourage privatization in the telecommunications industry in a manner beneficial to everyone in a society, not only to societal elites;
3. build and rely on simple tools that enhance the existing infrastructure as well as to evolve higher technologies on a step-by-step basis;
4. concentrate on providing public access in rural areas, community centers, and institutions;
5. rely on contents and applications developed in Africa that are socio-anthropologically driven to deal with the daunting tasks facing the continent; and
6. encourage research that will help to discern areas of technical applications or sociocultural needs as well as areas of training to maintain the existing infrastructures and teach the masses how to use these technologies. It is noteworthy to observe the proposed Nigerian information and communication is incorporating some of these proposals.

As Redner (2004) pointed out, it should be noted that ICTs have impacted international marketing in Nigeria and other developing countries because (a) they have impacted the development and creation of advertising messages that are disseminated worldwide instantly, thus assisting globalization of world economy; (b) the rapid dissemination and consumption of advertising has led to growing demand of consumer products and services; and (c) worldwide dissemination of advertising message is also impacting local values and cultures, with critics arguing that Western values are dominating or devaluing traditional values, which has lead to a backlash in the developing world.

The second primary research question in this study sought to discern the dominant cultural values and ideas conveyed in Nigerian mass media advertisements to discern their connotations and implication in the era of global marketing. To answer this question, 500-plus advertisements are examined to discover dominant (positive and negative) cultural values conveyed. As Table 7.2 demonstrates, a variety of cultural values were found. This analysis demonstrates that Nigerian advertisements use Western or traditional cultural values.

However, neither traditional nor Western values nor appeals are dominant. Two values (family and savings) serve as the most consistent forms of appeal used in Nigerian advertisements. Family is used often and relates to other values such as love, care, protection, and even savings. The study also finds that Nigerian mass media advertisements convey mainly positive values, such as love of nature, good health, service, truth, honesty, wisdom, endurance, and love.

When scholars discuss the social role of advertising in a developing nation, they are usually concerned with two issues—the cultural impact of advertising as it relates to consumption patterns and the effects on traditional values (Dagnino, 1980). Another issue deals with the effect of advertising on the mass media with regard to control and content (Janus, 1980, 1981; Schiller, 1977). Critics also claim that advertisers use Western values such as image, youth, individualism, and self-indulgence to promote their products (Leiss, Kline, & Jhally, 1990). However, this study does not establish whether domestic or foreign advertisers in Nigeria rely mainly on Western values for promotion. It finds that the most common appeals used in Nigerian advertising are savings, family, and information about products and services. Thus, it may be argued that advertising has no deleterious effects on Nigeria's traditional values (Ahmad, 1995).

Yet it should be noted that Western values such as individualism, image, youth, and snob are also used. Youth and image appeals are used extensively to promote smoking and beer drinking. When consumers in developing nations adopt these habits, they neglect traditional values (MacBride, 1980). Pairs of competitive values found in Malaysia as presented in Table 7.1, such as national unity, mutual respect, acceptance, and delayed gratification, are absent in the advertisements analyzed. Also absent from the advertisements are negative values such as extremism, defeatism, intolerance, prejudice, and mediocrity.

The relationship between advertising and mass media in developing countries remains an important social issue. Advertisements should be encouraged to promote the sale of goods and services; however, it also should incorporate values that will assist with the economic and social development of Nigeria and other Third World countries.

REFLECTIONS

During the past four decades, spurred by McLuhan's prediction of a "Global Village" made possible by technology and the growing importance of international marketing and communication in a shrinking world, studies on the role of advertising as it relates to culture have grown. Despite the increased interest in the subject, few, if any, studies have dealt with any African country (Al-Olayan & Karande, 2000; Harris & Attour, 2000). Few, if any, have examined the relationship and role between advertising and ICTs. This study serves an attempt to bridge that gap.

Guided by this premise, the discussions undertaken in this book regarding the role of ICTs and the values and symbols manifested in Nigerian mass media are multidimensional and complex. The answers provided serve as a vehicle for understanding the economic situation in Nigeria and other African countries in an era when international marketing has become the mainstay of the world economy. It could be argued that advertising cannot do without ICTs because these technologies are used in the creation, production, and delivery of the advertising artifacts. Like most products, manufacturer and service providers, manufacturers of ICTs, and corporations that use them to provide services need advertising to inform worldwide consumers about their availabilities and uses to create demand. Promoting awareness and creating demands help technologies to be diffused into societies globally. Thus, this development calls for a "balancing action" to ensure advertising does not become a vehicle that uses these technologies to disrupt the social, economic, and cultural basis off developing as critics have alleged both vehicles tend to produce.

According to Woods (1993), information and technologies are merging old distinctions among broadcasting, telephony, printing, and computing. Their interactive capacity and ability to communicate on demand in sound, pictures and graphics, as well as in script and numbers are upsetting and influence the cultural values, socioeconomic development, social relations, and government policies in the Third World. Advertising is one of the artifacts relayed through these innovations to the large audience in Africa and other parts of the Third World. Most of these innovations and artifacts are created in the North and relayed to South, thus the process remains a one-way street (Sussman, 1997).

These technical innovations, artifacts, messages, and values convey and influence changes worldwide, especially in the developing nations. It regenerates the debate of whether technology follows culture or culture follows technology (Herbig & Miller, 1992). Considering the increasing reliance on

ICTs and their role in international trade and communication as conduits for economic globalization, Nigeria and other developing nations must find ways to chart their economic development to compete in the global economy and promote the socioeconomic development of their peoples.

Reliance on Western models of development should be modified, if not abandoned, because of their introduction and perpetuation of Western values, distortion of their economies, creation of class divisions, and promotion of socioeconomic dependency. To help these nations, there is a need to conduct studies such as this to demystify the ideological and cultural bondage of the mass media and Western value and development models over the people and policy makers of the Third World. Such demystification will liberate, emancipate, and enlighten people in the Third World. The liberation will help consumers avoid remaining victimized by the forces of mass media, transnationals, and dominant elites in these countries. It may provide policymakers with ideas regarding the pursuit of home-grown economic development

Nigeria and other African nations can only achieve the goals of social modernization when they pursue true development. Proper development will occur when developing nations focus their economic destinies on their traditional values and national realities as Senghor (1964) advocates.

FUTURE RESEARCH

As one, if not the only, study that relies on qualitative approaches to examine the complex subjects of Nigeria's status with regard to the development of information and communication, and to what extent Nigerian advertisements embedded cultural values and symbols in their messages, this work represents a preliminary effort. It suggests this methodology could serve as a useful way to study the effectiveness of relying on mass media for social mobilization in Africa and other parts of the Third World. Results of such studies may help Third World governments as they formulate policies regarding the use of mass media and advertising in national development.

Future researchers may wish to examine the manifestation of cultural values and symbols from two African countries or among nations in other parts of the Third World. Such studies must attempt to determine which values are subjected to selective reinforcement and which suffer from neglect as Pollay (1990) suggests with the help of ICTs. Without a doubt, scholars who use this approach to elucidate the complex subtle advertising message as well as the role of ICTs in the Third World need to continue improving and refining it. In general, however, this research provides a positive direction for other researchers interested in illustrating subtextual messages and examining the role of advertising and ICTs in the economic development of Third World countries.

Appendix
Instrument (Cultural Analysis)

Name and Description of Product/Service:

What is (are) the dominant symbol(s) manifested in this advertisement?

The Meaning(s):

The Implication(s): Positive or Negative:

Relationship(s):

References

Abernethy, A., M. Franke, & R. George (1996). The information content of advertising: A meta-analysis. *Journal of Advertising* 25(2):1–17.

Adam, L. (1996). Electronic communications technology and development on internet in Africa. *Information Technology for Development* 7(3):133–144.

Africa Information Society Initiative (2001). About the African Information Society Initiative (AISI). [Online]. Available at http://www.bellanet.org/ Retrieved April 4, 2003.

Africa Recovery (1999a, December). Africa defines its electronic agenda. *Africa Recovery* 14(4):20.

Africa Recovery (1999b, December). Building blocks for communication. *Africa Recovery* 13(4):17.

Africa Recovery, (1999c, December), Forward steps at the African development forum. *Africa Recovery* 13(14):15.

Agbango, G. (1997). Political instability and economic development in sub-Saharan Africa. In G. Agbango (ed.), *Society and politics in Africa—Issues and trends in contemporary African politics: Stability, development and democratization* (pp. 13–51). New York: Peter Lang.

Agres, S., & T. Dubitsky (1996). Changing needs for brands. *Journal of Advertising Research* 27 (January/February): 21–30.

Ahmad, D. (1995). *Cultural imperialism through advertising: The case of advertising in Malaysia*. Unpublished Ph.D. dissertation, University of Nebraska at Lincoln.

Aihe, O. (2006, Jan. 2). GSM: Where will the next competition come from? *Vanguard Online*. [Online]. Available at http://www.vanguardngr.com Retrieved Jan. 3, 2006.

Aja, C. (1998, Nov. 11, 1998). Failed democratisation process blamed on poverty. *Post Express Wired*. [Online]. Available at http://www.postexpresswired.com/ Retrieved Nov. 14, 1998.

Ajayi, J. (2001, March 10). Challenges of advertising in Nigeria, by practitioner. *Vanguard*. [Online]. Available at http://www.vanguardngr.com March 10, 2001, is the date of retrieval, not actual date of publication. Actual date of publication was not stated on the printout.

Akinterinwa, B. (2001, Nov. 26). A rich country of poor people. *Asorock.com* [Online]. Available at http://www.asorock.com/newspub/ Retrieved Nov. 27, 2001.

Akor, A. (2001, Aug. 5). Nigeria to exhaust oil reserve in 29 years. *The Guardian Online*. [Online]. Available at http://www.ngrguadian.com/ Retrieved Aug. 7, 2001

Alaniz, M. L., & C. Wilkes (1995). Reinterpreting Latino culture in the commodity form: The case of alcohol advertising in the Mexican American community. *Hispanic Journal of Behavioral Science* 17(4):430--451.

Allenye, M. (1995). *International power and international communication.* New York: St. Martin's Press.

Al-Makaty, S., V. Norman, S. Whitlow, & D. Boyd (1996). Attitudes toward advertising in Islam. *Journal of Advertising Research* (May/June): 17–26.

Al-Olayan, F., & K. Karande (2000). A content analysis of magazine advertisements from the United States and the Arab world. *Journal of Advertising* 29(3):69–82.

Alozie, E. C. (2004). Review: *Advertising and society: Global issues. Journalism and Mass Communication Quarterly* 80(4):971–972.

Alozie, E. C. (2005a). Development and anti-development messages in Nigerian advertising. *The Journal of Development Communication* 15(2):13–31.

Alozie, E. C. (2005b). Review: Conserving cultures: technology, globalization, and the future of local cultures. *Journalism & Mass Communication Quarterly* 81(2):215–217.

Amaechi, K. (1997, Aug. 7–9). *Posturing advertising as an index of national planning and development.* Paper presented at Advertising Practitioners Council of Nigeria Executive Retreat on Advertising Policy and Strategic Planning, Ogere, Nigeria.

Amaizu, P. (2007, May 14, 2007). President Obasanjo and the 2007 [elections]. *The Guardian* [Online]. Available at http://www.guardiannewsngr.com. Retrieved June 27, 2007.

Amienyi, O. (1998). Nigeria. In A. Albarran & S. Chan-Olmsted (eds.), *Global media economics: Commercialization, concentration and integration of world media markets* (pp. 197–216). Ames: Iowa State University Press.

Amin, H., & L. Gher (2000). Digital communications in the Arab world entering the 21st Century. In L. Gher & H. Amin (eds.), *Civic course and digital communication in the Middle East* (pp. 109–140). Stamford, CT: Ablex

Amuzuo, C. (1999, Oct. 11). Advertising industry is in a state of stagnation—Nzeribe. *Vanguard.* [Online]. Available at http://www.vanguardngr.com/ Retrieved Oct. 12, 1999.

Amuzuo, C. (2000a, Feb. 14). Ad practitioners decry multiple vetting of advertisements. *Vanguard.* [Online]. Available at http://www.vanguardngr.com/ Retrieved Feb. 16, 2000.

Amuzuo, C. (2000b, April, 17). Modern advertising business thrives on diversification—Onyia. *Vanguard.* [Online]. Available at http://www.vanguardngr.com/ Retrieved April 20, 2000.

Anderson, M. (1984). *Madison Avenue in Asia: Politics and transnational advertising.* Cranbury, NJ: Associated University Press.

Anikulapo, J. (2001, Aug. 8). Mazrui lists dangers of globalization to Africa. *The Guardian Online.* [Online]. Available at http://www.ngrguardnews.com/ Retrieved Aug. 9 2001.

Anyigor, E. (1998, Nov. 25). Shonekan proffers recipe for stable democracy. *Post Express Wired.* [Online]. Available at http://www.postexpresswired.com/ Retrieved Nov. 28, 1998.

Arens, W. (2004). *Contemporary advertising* (9th ed.). Boston: McGraw-Hill.

Aronson, D. (1993). Why Africa stays poor and why it doesn't have to. *The Humanist* 53(2):9–14.

Asorock.com (2001, Nov. 2). Wishing away reality: Mbeki believes Africa will claim the 21st century. Asorock.com. [Online]. Available at http://www.asorock.com/ Retrieved Nov. 2, 2001.

Associated Press (1993, July 9). *Religion, tribe, the dynamics of Nigerian politics.*

Ayeoyenikan, S. (2001, March 27). Plans agency for IT implementation. *The Guardian Online.* [Online]. Available at http://ngrguardiannews.com Retrieved March 2, 2001.

Ayittey, G. (1997). Obstacles to African development. In G. Agbango (ed.), *Society and politics in Africa—Issues and trends in contemporary African politics: Stability, development and democratization* (pp. 321–331). New York: Peter Lang.

Aziken, E. (2001, June 6). 70m Nigerians are poor. Asorock.com. [Online]. Available at http://www/asorock.com/newspub/ Retrieved June 2, 2001.

Azikiwe, N. (1969). *Renascent Africa*. New York: Negro Universities Press.

Balit, S. (1996). Toward national communication-for-development policies in Africa. [Online]. Available at http:www.fao.WAICENTI/FAOINFO/SUSTDEV Retrieved Feb. 15, 1998.

Batra, A., J. Myers, & D. Aaker (1996). *Advertising management* (5th ed.). Upper Saddle, NJ: Prentice Hall.

Baumgart, W. (1982). *Imperialism: The idea and reality of British and French colonial expansion, 1880–1914*. London: Oxford University Press.

BBC (2007, May 14).China launches Nigerian Satellite. [Online].Available at http://news.bbc.co.uk/1/hi/world/africa/6653067.stm. Retrieved June 27, 2007.

BBC News (2006, April 21). Nigeria settles Paris Club debt. BBC News. [Online]. Available at http://news.bbc.co.uk/2/hi/business/4926966.stm. Retrieved July 22, 2007.

Bentsi-Enchill, N. (1999). Cool heads and new technology: First African development forum tackles continent's telecommunication issues. *Africa Recovery* 13(4):13.

Berg, B. (2001). *Qualitative research methods for the social sciences*. Needham Heights, MA: Allyn & Bacon.

Bernstein, D. (1972). What advertising is. In M. Smelt (ed.), *What advertising is* (pp. 10–38). London: Pelham Books Ltd.

Bertelsen, E. (1996). Selling change: Advertisements for the 1994 South African election. *African Affairs* 95:225–252.

Bitterman, M. (1985). Mass media and social change. *Media Asia* 2(1):38–43.

Boafo, S. (1985). Utilizing development communication strategies in African societies: A critical perspective (development communication in Africa. *Gazette* 35:83–92.

Boafo, S. (1991). Communication technology and dependent development in sub-Saharan Africa. In G. Sussman & J. Lent (eds.), *Transnational communication: Wiring the world* (pp. 103–149). Newbury Park, CA: Sage.

Boddewyn, J., R. Soehl, & J. Picard (1986). Standardization in international marketing: Is Ted Levitt in fact right? *Business Horizons* 29:69–75.

Bourgault, L. (1995). *Mass media in sub-Saharan Africa*. Bloomington, IN: Indiana University Press.

Boyd-Barrett, O. (1995). The political economy approach. In O. Boyd-Barrett & C. Newbold (eds.), *Approaches to media: A reader* (pp. 186–192). London: Arnold.

Boyd-Barrett, O. (2002). Theory in media research. In C. Newbold, O. Boyd-Barrett, & H. Bulck (eds.), *The media handbook* (pp. 1–54). London: Arnold.

Brummett, B. (1994). *Rhetoric in popular culture*. New York: St. Martin's Press.

Buzzell, R. (1968). Can you standardize multinational marketing? *Harvard Business Review* 49(November–December):102–113.

Cardoso, F. (1977). The consumption of dependency theory in the United States. *Latin American Research Review* 12(3):7–24.

Carey, J. (1989). *Communication as culture: Essays on media and society*. Boston: Unwin Hyman.

Carr, E. (1939). *The twenty years' crisis*. London: Macmillan.

Chen, G., & W. Starosta (1998). Foundations of intercultural communication. Boston: Allyn & Bacon.

Cheng, H. (1997). Toward an understanding of cultural values manifest in advertising: A content analysis of Chinese television advertising commercials in 1990 and 1995. *Journalism & Mass Communication Quarterly* 74(4):773–796.

Cheng, H., & J. Schweitzer (1996). Cultural values reflected in Chinese and U.S. television commercials. *Journal of Advertising Research* 36(3):27–45.

Chinweizu (1993, April 27–29). Reparations and new global order: A comparative overview. Paper Presented at the Second Plenary Session of the First Pan-African Conference on Reparations, Abuja, Nigeria.

Clarke, J. (1995). Introduction. In J. Jackson (ed.), *Introduction to African civilizations* (pp. 3–35). New York: Citadel Press.

CNN.com (2001, Jan. 25). Social forum seeks alternative agenda. [Online]. Available at http://www.cnn.com/2001/world Retrieved Jan. 26, 2005.

CNN International.com (2007, April 25). Nigeria's Obasanjo defends election. [Online]. Available athttp://www.cnn.com/2007/WORLD/africa/04/25/nigeria.elections/index. Retrieved June 27, 2007.

Collins, C. (2007, 2007, May 9). Ngige, Ukachukwu file petitions at election tribunal. *The Guardian* [Online]. Available athttp://www.guardiannewsngr.com. Retrieved June 27, 2007.

Comeliau, C. (1995). The development debate. *UNESCO Courier* 48(10):20.

Dagnino, E. (1980). Cultural and ideological dependence: Building a theoretical framework. In K. Kumar (ed.), *Transnational enterprises: Their impact on Third World societies and cultures* (pp. 297–322). Boulder, CO: Westview Press.

Davidson, L. (1999). Connecting with African Diaspora. *Africa Recovery* 13(4):16.

De Beer, A, F. Kasoma, E. Megwa, & E. Steyn (1995). Sub-Saharan Africa. In J. Merrill (ed,), *Global journalism: Survey of international Communicatio* (3rd ed., pp. 209–268). White Plains, NY: Longman.

Deji-Folutile, B., E. Amaefule, & O. Ezeobi (2007, May 14). Nigeria launches new satellite in China. *Punch on the Web.* [Online].Available at http://www.punchng.com/ Retrieved June 27, 2007.

Domatob, J. (1987). Ethical implication of transnational corporation advertising in sub-Saharan Africa. In J. Domatob, A. Jika, & I. Nwosu (eds.), *Mass media and the African society* (pp. 281–295). Nairobi, Kenya: The African Council on Communication Education.

Domatob, J. (1988). Sub-Saharan Africa's media and neo-colonialism. *Africa Media Review* 3(1):149–173.

Douglas, S., & B. Dubois (1977). Looking at the cultural environment of international marketing. *Columbia Journal of World Business* 12:102–109.

Douglas, S., & Y. Wind (1987). The myth of globalization. *Columbia Journal of World Business* 4(Winter):19–28.

Dyer, G. (1982). *Advertising as communication.* London: Methuen.

Ebhodaghe, S. (2001, Feb. 20). New IT policy underway. *The Guardian Online.* [Online]. Available at http://ngrguardiannews.com Retrieved Feb. 21, 2001.

Ebhodaghe, S. (2001, Jan. 30). How the [IT] Sector can grow, by experts. *The Guardian Online.* [Online]. Available at http://ngrguardiannews.com Retrieved Feb. 21, 2001.

Ebonugwo, M., & S. Ogbeifun (2001, May 9). OAU has not failed—Åhmed. *Vanguard.* [Online]. Available at http://www.vanguardngr.com. Retrieved May 10, 2001.

Economic Commission for Africa (1998, May 11–13). Report on a workshop on national information and communication infrastructures (NICI) strategy for Namibia. Presentation at Windhoek, Namibia. [Online]. Available at http://www.bellanet.org. Retrieved March 10, 2001.

ECOWAS Official Site (2001). Achievement of ECOWAS: Development of physical infrastructures for road, telecommunication and energy. [Online]. Available at http://www.ecowas.int.sitecedeao Retrieved March 10, 2001.

Electronic Mail and Guardian (1998, May 18). Why are the poor picking up the tab? [Online]. Available at http://www.mg.co.za/mg/news_htm Retrieved March 10, 2001.

Electronic Mail and Guardian (1998, Nov. 4). Africa's debt cow is milked dry. [Online]. Available at http://www.mg.co.za/mg/news_htm Retrieved March 10, 2001.

Elinder, E. (1965). How international can European advertising be? *Journal of Marketing* 29(April):7–11.

Embassy of Nigeria (1998, May 8). The economy of Nigeria. [Online]. Available at http://www.tribeca.ios.com/ Retrieved May 10, 1998.

Enyinnaya, B. (1998, Aug. 19). Government earns $250b from oil. *Post Express Wired*. [Online]. Available at http://www.postexpresswired.com/postexpress. Retrieved Aug. 25, 1998.

Eribo, F. (2001). *In search of greatness: Russia communications with Africa and the world*. Westport, CT: Ablex.

Fadeiye, D. (1978). *Current affairs essays on social studies (based on Nigerian and Africa)*. Imo, Ilesha, Nigeria: Ilesanmi Press & Sons (Nig.) Ltd.

Famoroti, B. (2005, Feb. 1). New year advert lull: Telecoms, others to the rescue. *Punch on the Web*. [Online]. Available at http://www.punchng.com/ Retrieved Feb. 2005.

Faringer, G. (1991). *Press freedom in Africa*. New York: Praeger.

Fatt, A. (1967). The danger of "local" international advertising. *Journal of Marketing* 31(January):60–62.

Fejes, F. (1980). The growth of multinational advertising agencies in Latin America. *Journal of Communication* 30(4):36–49.

Firat, A., & A. Venkatesh (1995). Liberatory postmodernism and the reenchantment of consumption. *Journal of Consumer Research* 22(December):239–267.

Fiske, J. (1992). British cultural studies and television. In R. Allen (ed.), *Channels of discourse, reassembled: Television and contemporary criticism* (pp. 284–326). Chapel Hill, NC: The University of North Carolina Press.

Fortner, R. (1993). *International communication: History, conflict, and control of the global metropolis*. Belmont, CA: Wadsworth.

Freire, P. (1993). *Pedagogy of the oppressed* (Myra B. Ramos, Trans.). New York: Continuum.

Frith, K. (1996). Dependence or convergence? In K. Frith (ed.), *Advertising in Asia: communication, consumption, and culture* (pp. 3–10). Ames: Iowa State University Press.

Frith, K. (1997). Preface (p. xiii) and undressing the ad: Reading culture in advertising. In K. Frith (ed.), *Undressing the ad: Reading culture in advertising* (pp. 1–17).. New York: Peter Lang.

Frith, K., & M. Frith (1990). Western advertising and Eastern culture: The confrontation in Southeast Asia. *Current Issues and Research in Advertising* 12(1–2):63–73.

Frith, K., & B. Mueller (2003). *Advertising and society: Global issues*. New York: Peter Lang.

Frith, K.T., & D. Wesson (1991). A comparison of cultural values in British and American print advertising: A study of magazines. *Journalism Quarterly* 68(1/2):216–223.

Gaile, G., & A. Ferguson (1996). Success in African social development: Some positive indications. *Third World Quarterly* 17(3):557–572.

Galtung, J. (1971). A structural theory of imperialism. *Journal of Peace Research* 8(2):81–117.

Galtung, J. (1980). *The true worlds: A transnational perspective.* New York: The Free Press.

Garreau, J. (1981). *The nine nations of North America.* Boston: Houghton Mifflin.

George, A., & C. Ogbondah (1999). The Ogoni crisis: A critical analysis of Nigeria's military junta's international image-laundering campaign. *Southwestern Mass Communication Journal* 15(1):73–89.

Gershon, R. (1997). *The transnational media corporation: Global messages and free market competition.* Mahwah, NJ: Lawrence Erlbaum Associates.

Gifford, A. (1993, April 27–29). *The legal basis for the claim of reparations.* Paper presented at the Second Plenary Session of the First Pan-African Conference on Reparations, Abuja, Nigeria.

Goonasekera, A. (1995). Asian viewers do not see western programmes as corrupting their cultures. *Media Asia* 22(4):217–221.

Gramsci, A. (1971). *Selections from prison notebooks* (Q. Hoare and G. Nowell-Smith, Eds. and Trans.). New York: International Universities Press.

Griffin, C. (1995). Teaching rhetorical criticism with Thelma and Louise. *Communication Education* 44(2):165.

Grosswiler, P. (2004). Continuing media controversies. In A. de Beer & J. Merrill (eds.), *Global journalism: Topical issues and media systems* (4th ed., pp. 112–127). Boston: Allyn & Bacon.

Guttsman, J. (1997, Oct. 31). *Aid for a wounded Tiger: Group offers Indonesia loans up to $40 billion.* Reuters News Service. [Online]. Available at http://www.chron.com/content/chronicle/business Retrieved Nov. 1, 1997.

Hachten, W. (1993). *The growth of the media in the Third World: African failures and Asian successes.* Ames: Iowa State University Press.

Hall, E. (1959). *The silent language.* Garden City, NY: Doubleday.

Hall, E., & M. Hall (1990). *Understanding cultural differences.* Yarmouth, ME: Intercultural Press.

Hall, S. (1977). Culture, the media and the "ideological effect." In J. Curran, M. Gurevitch, & J. Woollacott (eds.), *Mass communication and society* (pp. 315–348). London: Open University Press/Edward Arnold.

Hall, S. (1980). Encoding and decoding. In S. Hall, D. Hobson, A. Lowe, & P. Willis (eds.), *Culture, media and language* (pp. 128–138). London: Hutchinson.

Hamelink, C. (1997). MacBride with hindsight. In P. Golding & P. Harris (eds.), *Beyond cultural imperialism: Globalization, communication and the New international order* (pp. 68–92). Thousand Oaks, CA. Sage.

Haque, M. (1993). Information societies and the developing world: A synthesis of theories. *Monograph Number 3.* Athens, GA: University of Georgia.

Harris, G., & S. Attour (2000). Content analysis of advertising 1970–1997: A review of and assessment of methodologies. In S. Monye (ed.), *The handbook of international marketing communications* (pp. 237–263). Oxford, England: Blackwell.

Hawk, B. (1992). Introduction: Metaphors of African coverage. In Beverly Hawk (ed.), *Africa's Media Image* (pp. 3–15). New York: Praeger.

Herbig, A., & J. Miller (1992). Culture and technology: Does traffic flow both directions. *Journal of Global Marketing* 6(3):75–102.

Hofstede, G. (1980). *Culture's consequences: International differences in work-related values.* Beverly Hills, CA: Sage.

Hofstede, G. (1983). Dimensions of national cultures in fifty countries and three regions. In J. B. Deregowski, S. Dziurawiec, & R. C. Annis (eds.), *Expectations in cross-cultural psychology* (pp. 335–355). Lisse, Netherlands: Swets & Zeitlinger.

Hout, T., M. Porter, & E. Rudden (1982). How global companies win out. *Harvard Business Review* 60(September–October):98–108.

Hudson, R., & J. Ozanne (1988). Alternative ways of seeking knowledge in consumer research. *Journal of Consumer Research* 14:508–521.

Hughes, T. (2000). Technological momentum. In A. Teich (ed.), *Technology and the future*. Boston: Bedford/St. Martin's.

Hyun, C. (1990). *Transnationalization of Korean advertising: A qualitative and quantitative analysis*. Unpublished Ph.D. dissertation, University of Minnesota at Minneapolis.

Ihonvbere, J. (1997a). Democratization in Africa: Challenges and prospects. In G. Agbango (ed.), *Society and politics in Africa—issues and trends in contemporary African politics: Stability, development and* democratization (pp. 287–320). New York: Peter Lang.

Ihonvbere, J. (1997b). Pan Africanism: Agenda for African Unity in the 1990s? In G. Agbango (ed.), *Society and politics in Africa—issues and trends in contemporary African politics: Stability, development and democratization* (pp. 337–366). New York: Peter Lang.

Ikeh, G. (1999, July 22). ECOWAS, ITU sign agreement. PANA. [Online]. Available at http://www.allafrica.com Retrieved June 20, 2001.

Inayatullah (1967). Towards a non-Western model of development. In D. Lerner & W. Schramm (eds.), *Communication and change in the developing nations* (pp. 99–102). Honolulu: East-West Center Press.

Inayatullah (1976). Towards a non-western model of development. In D. Lerner & W. Schramm (eds.), *Communication and change in the developing nations* (pp. 99–102). Honolulu: East-West Center Press.

Isar, R. (1996). Javier Perez de Cuellar: Our creative Diversity. *The UNESCO Courier* 49(8):4–7.

Jain, S. (1993). *Marketing planning and strategy*. Cincinnati, OH: Thomson-Southwestern Publishing.

James, W., & J. Hill (1991). International advertising manager: To adaptor not to adapt. *Journal of Marketing* 31(3):65–71.

Janus, N. (1980). The making of the global consumer: Transnational advertising and the mass media in Latin America. *Dissertation Abstracts International* 41–08, Section A:3310.

Janus, N. (1981). Advertising and the mass media in the era of global corporation. In E. McAnany, J. Schnitman, & N. Janus (eds.), *Communication and social structure: Critical studies in mass media research* (pp. 287–316). New York: Praeger.

Janus, N. (1986). Transnational advertising: Some considerations on the impact of peripheral societies. In A. Rita & E. McAnany (eds.), *Communication and Latin America society: Trends in critical research, 1960–1985* (pp. 127–142). Madison, WI: University of Wisconsin.

Janus, N., & R. Roncagliolo (1979). Advertising, mass media and dependency. *Development Dialogue* 1:81–97.

Jensen, M. (1998, December). Internet open new markets for Africa. *Africa Recovery* 12(13):6.

Jensen, M. (2000, November). *African Internet connectivity—The African Internet—A status report*. [Online]. Available at http;//www3.sn.apc.org/ Retrieved Nov. 3, 2001.

Jun, Y. (1994). *Cross-cultural content of advertising: A comparative analysis of the United States and Korea*. [Unpublished] University of Southern Mississippi, Hattiesburg, MI.

Kanso, A. (1986). Management perceptions of culture in international advertising: A survey of culture in American corporations. *Dissertation Abstract International* 47/05:1522.

Karuppur, D. (1995). Marketing strategies in global markets: A transaction cost analysis. *Dissertation Abstracts International* 55–07, Section A:1802.

Katembo, B. (2001, Feb. 12–17). Roots, videoconferencing, and Afrocentricity. Presentation at the Conference of National Association of African American Studies, National Association of Hispanic and Latin Studies, National Association of Native American Studies and International Association of Asian Studies, Houston, TX.

Keegan, W. (1989). *Global marketing.* Englewood Cliffs, NJ: Prentice Hall.

Keillor, B., R. Parker, & A. Schaefer (1996). Influences on adolescent brand preferences in the United States and Mexico. *Journal of Advertising Research* 36(3, May/June):47–57.

Kellner, D. (1988). Reading images critically: Toward a postmodern pedagogy. *Journal of Education* 170(3):31–52.

Kerlinger, F. (1986). *Foundations of behavioral research.* New York: Holt, Rinehart & Winston.

Kirkpatrick, J. (1990). A philosophic defense of advertising. In R. Hovland & G. Wilcox (eds.), *Advertising in society: Classic and contemporary readings on advertising role in society* (pp. 508–522). Lincolnwood, IL: NTC Business Books.

Korie, A. (1997, April, 4). Shell replies World Council of Churches. *Post Express Wired.* [Online]. Available at http://www.postexpresswired.com. Retrieved Aug. 10, 1998.

Kotler, P. (1986). Global standardization—courting danger. *Journal of Consumer Marketing* 3(2):13–15.

Kumar, K. (1980). Social and cultural impact of transnational enterprises: An overview. In K. Kumar (ed.), *Transnational enterprises: Their impact on Third World societies and cultures* (pp. 1–38). Boulder, CO: Westview Press.

Lancet (1997, Jan. 11). A good turn for Africa, please. 349(9045):69.

Lane, W., K. King, & J. Russell (2005). *Kleppner's advertising rocedure* (16th ed.). Upper Saddle River, NJ: Pearson/Prentice Hall.

Langrehr, F. W., & C. L. Caywood (1989). An assessment of the "sins" and "virtues" portrayed in advertising. *International Journal of Advertising* 8:391–403.

LaPalombara, J. (1979). *Multinational corporations and developing countries.* Report No. 767. New York: Conference Board, Inc.

Leiss, W., S. Kline, & S. Jhally (1990). *Social communication in advertising: Persons, products and images of well-being* (2nd ed.). New York: Routledge.

Lerner, D. (1963). Toward a communication theory of modernization: A set of considerations. In L. Pye (ed.), *Communication and political development* (pp. 327–350). Princeton, NJ: Princeton University Press.

Levitt, T. (1983). The globalization of markets. *Harvard Business Review* (May–June): 61, 92–102.

Lexis-Nexis (2001, Oct. 22). Country: Nigeria. *Lexis-Nexis Academic Universe–Document.* [Online]. Available at http://www.tribeca.ios.com/ Retrieved Oct. 25, 2001.

Lin, C. (2001). Cultural values reflected in Chinese and American television advertising. *Journal of Advertising* 30(4):83––94.

Logie, D. (1996, Feb. 17). Africa's leaders appeal for help with debt crisis. *British Medical Journal* 312(7028):399.

Lorimer, R., & M. Gasher, (2001). *Mass communication in Canada* (4th ed.). Oxford: Oxford University Press.

MacBride, S. (1980). *Many voices, one world: Communication and society, today and tomorrow.* New York: UNESCO.

MacKay, I. (1964). *Broadcasting in Nigeria.* Ibadan, Nigeria: University Press.

Mamdani, M. (1998, Nov. 2). Why foreign invaders can't help Congo. *Electronic Mail and Guardian.* [Online]. Available at http://www.mg.co.za/mg/newscom Retrieved March 10, 2001.

Mandell, M. (1984). *Advertising* (4th ed.). Englewood Cliffs, NJ: Prentice Hall.

Martin, R., S. Chaffee, & F. Izcaray (1979). Media and consumerism in Venezuela. *Journalism Quarterly* 56(2):296–335.

Martins, L. (1982). The state-transnational corporation-local entrepreneur joint venture in Brazil: How to relax and enjoy a forced marriage. In H. Makler, A. Martinelli, & N. Smelser (eds.), *The new international economy* (pp. 261–286). Beverly Hills, CA: Sage.

Mazrui, A. (1995). *The African condition: A political diagnosis* (rev. ed.). Cambridge, UK: Cambridge University Press.

Mbendi (1997, Sept. 4). Nigeria—Telecommunication industry. Researched and prepared for Mbendi AfroPaedia by the African Development Consulting Group. [Online]. Available at http://www.mbendi.co.za/adcg/ Retrieved Oct. 10, 1999.

Mbendi (1998, Oct. 10). Stanbic Merchant Bank Nigeria Limited. Nigeria. Economic Indicators. [Online]. Available at http://www.mbendi.co.za/stanbic Retrieved Oct. 10, 1999.

McCarty, J. (1994). The role of international cultural value orientations in cross-cultural research and international marketing and advertising. In B. Englis (ed.), *Global and multinational advertising* (pp. 23–45). Hillsdale, NJ: Lawrence Erlbaum Associates.

McChesney, R. (2001). Global media, neoliberalism and imperialism. *Monthly Review* 52(10):1–15.

McGeary, J., & M. Michaels (1998, March, 30). Africa rising. *Time*, pp. 30–46.

McLuhan, M. (1964). *Understanding media*. New York: McGraw-Hill.

McNelly, J. (1968). Perspectives on the role of mass communication in the national development. In J. McNelly & D. Berlo (eds.), *Mass communication and development of Nations* (pp. 11–112). East Lansing, MI: Michigan State University.

McPhail, T. (1987). *Electronic colonialism: The future of international broadcasting and communication*. Newbury Park, CA: Sage.

McPhail, T. L. (2006). *Global communication: Theories, stakeholders, and trends*. Malden, MA: Blackwell.

Mendelssohn, K. (1976). *The secret of Western domination*. New York: Praeger.

Ministry of Communications—Ghana (2001, June 3). Economic Commission for Africa forum for the development of Africa: Plan for national information and communications infrastructure of Ghana, 2000–2005. [Online]. Available at http://www.bellanet.org. Date reflects when the information was obtained from the Internet. Retrieved Oct. 10, 2001.

Moemeka, A. (1994). Development communication: A historical and conceptual overview. In A. Moemeka (ed.), *Communicating for development: A new pan-disciplinary perspective* (pp. 3–22). Albany, NY: State University of New York Press.

Moemeka, A. (1997). Communalistic societies: Community and self-respect as African values. In C. Christians & M. Traber (eds.), *Communication ethics and universal values* (pp. 170–193). Thousand Oaks, CA: Sage.

Moriarty, S., & T. Duncan (1990). Global advertising: Issues and practices. *Current Issues and Research in Advertising* 13:313–341.

Mosco, V. (1995). *The political economy tradition of media research, module 1 unit 4 of the MA in Mass Communication*. Leicester: University of Leicester.

Mowlana, H. (1996). *Global communication in transition: The end of diversity?* Thousand Oaks, CA: Sage.

Mueller, B. (1987). Reflections of culture: An analysis of Japanese and American advertising appeals. *Journal of Advertising* 27(3):51–59.

Mueller, B. (1996). *International advertising: Communicating across culture*. Belmont, CA: Wadsworth.

Mueller, B. (2004). *Dynamics of international advertising: Theoretical and practical perspectives*. New York: Peter Lang.

Murdock, G. (1955). The common denominator of cultures. In R. Linton (ed.), *The science of man in the world crisis* (pp. 123–142). New York: Columbia University Press.

Mutizwa, G. (2000, Nov. 22). New economy leaves Africa in dust. Reuters. [Online]. Available at http://www.zdnet.com Retrieved June 10, 2001.

Mwaura, P. (1998). Africa connects to the internet. *Africa Recovery* 11(4):22.

National Public Radio (1999, May 22). *Weekend All Things Considered*. KBIA 91.3, Columbia, Missouri.

Ndukwe, E. (2006, Jan. 2). Furthering the digital revolution in Nigeria in era of technology convergence. *Vanguard Online*. [Online]. Available at http://www.vanguardngr.com Retrieved Jan. 3, 2006.

Neal, R. (1998, August). Bridging the telecommunication gap. *Africa Recovery* 12(1):38.

Newsom, D. (2004). Global advertising and public relations. In A. de Beer & J. Merrill (eds.), *Global journalism: Topical issues and media systems* (4th ed., pp. 93–101). Boston: Allyn & Bacon.

Ngugi, M. (1995). Development communication: A clarification constructs. *Africa Media Review* 9(20):1–15.

Ngwainmbi, E. (1995). *Communication efficiency and rural development in Africa: The case of Cameroon*. New York: University Press of America.

Ngwainmbi, E. (1999). *Exporting communication technology to developing countries*. Lanham, MD: University Press of America.

Nkwocha, J. (2007, July 22). Post-debt relief: What next? *Vanguard*. [Online]. Available at http://www.vanguardngr.com/articles. Retrieved July 22, 2007.

Nwachukwu, C. (1999, July, 13). UNDP ranks Nigeria low in development. *Post Express Wired*. [Online]. Available at http://www.postexpresswired.com Retrieved July 14 12, 1999.

Nwosu, I. (1990). Public relations and advertising in the process of governance and economic recovery in Nigeria. In I. Nwosu (ed.), *Mass communication and national development—perspectives on the communication environments of development in Nigeria* (pp. 231–242). Aba: Frontier Publishers.

Nyamnjoh, F. (1999). Africa and the information highway: The need for mitigated euphoria. *Ecquid Novi* 20(1):31–49.

Nye, J. S. (1990). Soft power. *Foreign Policy* 80(Fall):153–171.

Obadina, T. (2000, July 20). Blame Africa's woes on Africans. *Vanguard*. [Online]. Available at http://www.vanguardngr.com/ Retrieved July 21, 2000.

Obeng-Quaidoo, I. (1986). A proposal for new communication research methodologies in Africa. *Africa Media Review* 1(1):89–-98.

Odili, P. (2007, June 1). Gaps in Yar'Adua's inaugural speech. *Vanguard Online*. [Online]. Available at http://www.vanguardngr.com Retrieved June 27, 2007.

Okigbo, C. (1989). Communications ethics and social Change: A Nigerian perspective. In T. Cooper, C. Christians, F. Plude, & R. White (eds.), *Communication ethics and global change* (pp. 124–135). White Plains, NY: Longman.

Oladipo, O. (1995). Reason, identity, and the African quest: The problems of self-definition in African philosophy. *Africa Today* 42(3):39–64.

Olaniran, B., & R. Roach (1994). Communication apprehension and classroom apprehension in Nigerian classrooms. *Communication Quarterly* 42(2):379.

Ollor-Obari, J. (1999, June 20). Rivers to flush out ghost workers. *The Guardian Online*. [Online]. Available at http://www.ngrguardiannews.com/Retrieved June 22, 1999.

Onkvisit, S., & J. Shaw (1987). Standardized international advertising: A review and critical evaluation of the theoretical and empirical evidence. *Columbia Journal of World* Business 22(Fall):43–55.

Onuorah, M. (2001, Dec. 20). Govt[.] to reschedule debts with Germany, two others. *The Guardian Online.* [Online]. Available at http://www.ngrguadian.com/ Retrieved Dec. 22, 2001.

Opubor, A. (1986). Mass communication and modern development in Nigeria. In O. Nwuneli (ed.), *Mass communication in Nigeria: A book of readings* (pp. 183–200). Enugu, Nigeria: Fourth Dimension Publishers.

Ostheimer, J. (1973). *Nigerian politics.* New York: Harper & Row.

Pajnik, M., & P. Lesjak-Tusek (2002). Observing discourse of advertising: Mobitel's interpellation of potential consumers. *Journal of Communication Inquiry* 26(3):277–299.

Parekh, B. (1997). National culture and multiculturalism. In K. Thompson (ed.), *Media and cultural regulation* (pp. 163–205). London: Sage.

Pasqua, T. M., R. E. Buckalew, J. K. Rayfied, & J. W. Tankard (1990). *Mass media in the information age.* Englewood Cliffs, NJ: Prentice Hall.

People's Daily Online (2005, Jan. 5). Nigeria to settle all Paris Club debt by March 2006: Obasanjo. *People's Daily Online.* [Online]. Available at http:// english.peopledaily.com.cn/200601/05/eng20060105_232978.html Retrieved July 23, 2007.

Petras, J. (1998). Che Guevara and contemporary revolutionary movements. *Latin American Perspectives* 25(4):9–18.

Pfaff, W. (1995). A new colonialism: Europe must go back into Africa. *Foreign Affairs* (January/February):2–6.

Pollay, R. (1990). The distorted mirror: Reflections on the unintended consequences of advertising. In R. Hovland & G. Wilcox (eds.), *Advertising in society: Classic and contemporary readings on advertising role in society* (pp. 437–476). Lincolnwood, IL: NTC Business Books.

Pollay, R., & K. Gallagher (1990). Advertising and cultural values: Reflections in the distorted mirror. *International Journal of Advertising* 9:359–372.

Post Express Wired (1998, Dec. 21). NURTW chief urges govt[.] to ban sale of alcohol in motorparks. [Online]. Available at http://www.postexpresswired. com Retrieved Dec. 23, 1998.

Pratt, C. (1996). Africa south of the Sahara. In P. Jeter, K. Rampal, V. Cambridge, & C. Pratt (ed.), *International Afro mass media: A reference guide* (pp. 3–61). Westport, CT: Greenwood.

Prebble, J. (1992). Global expansion: The case of US fast-food franchisors. *Journal of Global Marketing* 6(1/2):185–205.

Quelch, J., & E. Hoff (1986). Customizing global marketing. *Harvard Business Review* 64(3, May–June):59–68.

Raufu, A. (2003). Nigeria's satellite launch gets mixed reaction. *SciDev.Net.* [Online]. Available at http://www.scidev.net/news/ Retrieved June 27, 2007.

Redner, H. (2004). *Conserving culture: Technology, globalization and the future of local cultures.* Lanham, MD: Rowan & Littlefield.

Rijkens, R. (1992). *European advertising strategies.* London: Cassell.

Roberts, T. E. (1987). Mass communication, advertising and popular culture: Propagators and procedures of consumer behavior and ideology. In J. Domatob, A. Jika, & I. Nwosu (eds.), *Mass media and the African society* (pp. 269–280). Nairobi, Kenya: African Council on Communication Education.

Robertson, R. (1992). *Globalization: Social theory and global culture.* Thousand Oak, CA: Sage.

Rodney, W. (1974). *How Europe underdeveloped Africa.* Washington, DC: Howard University Press.

Rogers, E. (1976). Communication and development: The passing of the dominant paradigm. In E. Rogers (ed.), *Communication and development: Critical perspectives* (pp. 213–240). Beverly Hills, CA: Sage.

Roncagliolo, R. (1986). Transnational communication and culture. In R. Atwood & E. McAnany (eds.), *Communication and Latin America: Trends in critical research, 1960–1985* (pp. 79–88). Madison: University of Wisconsin.

Roncagliolo, R., & N. Janus (1981). Advertising and the democratization of communication. *Development Dialogue* 2:38–39.

Salinas, R., & L. Paldan (1979). Culture in the process of dependent development: Theoretical perspectives. In K. Nordenstreng & H. Schiller (eds.), *National sovereignty and international communication* (pp. 82–98). Norwood, NJ: Ablex.

Samovar, L., & R. Porter (1994). An introduction to intercultural communication. In L. Samovar & R. Porter (eds.), *Intercultural communication, A reader* (7th ed., pp. 4–36). Belmont, CA: Wadsworth.

Sandage, C. (1990). Some institutional aspects of advertising. In R. Hovland & G. Wilcox (eds.), *Advertising in society: Classic and contemporary readings on advertising role in society* (pp. 3–10). Lincolnwood, IL: NTC Business Books.

Sarti, I. (1981). Communication and cultural dependency: A misconception. In E. McAnany, J. Schnitman, & N. Janus (eds.), *Communication and social structure: Critical studies in mass media research* (pp. 317–334). New York: Praeger.

Sauvant, K. (1976). Multinational enterprises and the transmission of cultures: The international supply of advertising services and business education. *Journal of Peace Research* 12(1):49–65.

Schiller, H. (1970). *Mass communication and American empire.* New York: Augustus M. Kelley.

Schiller, H. (1977). Transnational media and national development. In J. Richstad (ed.), *New perspectives in international communication* (pp. 33–43). Honolulu: East-West Communication Institute.

Schiller, H. (1979). Transnational media and national development. In K. Nordenstreng & H. Schiller (eds.), *National sovereignty and international communication* (pp. 21–32). Norwood, NJ: Ablex.

Schudson, M. (1984). *Advertising, the uneasy persuasion: Its dubious impact on American society.* New York: Basic Books.

Segal-Horn, S., and H. Davison (1992). Global markets, the global consumer and international retailing. *Journal of Global Marketing* 5(3):31–61.

Sen, A. (1996). A matter of choice. *The UNESCO Courier* 49(8):10–13.

Senghor, L. (1964). *On African socialism* (Mercer Cook, Trans.). New York: Praeger.

Servaes, J. (1991). Toward a new perspectives for communication and development. In F. Casmir (ed.), *Communication in development* (pp. 51–85). Norwood, NJ: Ablex.

Singer, M., & A. Wildavasky (1996). *The real world order: Zones of peace and zones of turmoil* (rev. ed.). Chattam, NJ: Chattam House Publishers.

Sinha, A. (1986). Communication and rural development: The Indian scene. *Gazette* 38:59–70.

Smith, A. (1980). *The geopolitics of information: How western cultures dominates the world.* New York: Oxford University Press.

Solomon, L. (1978). *Multinational corporations and the emerging world order.* Port Washington, NY: Kennikat Press.

Sorenson, R., & U. Weichman (1975). How multinationals view standardization. *Harvard Business Review* 53(3):59–68.

Sreberny-Mohammadi, A. (1997). The many cultural faces of imperialism. In P. Golding & P. Harris (eds.), *Beyond cultural imperialism: Globalization, communication and the new International order* (pp. 48–67). Thousand Oaks, CA: Sage.

Stafford, M. (2005). International services advertising (ISA). *Journal of Advertising* 34(1):65–86.

Stern, B. (1988). How does an ad mean? Language in services advertising. *Journal of Advertising* 17(2):3–14.

Stewart, I. (1997, June 22). Workers speak pp in Vietnam. *Associated Press.* [Online]. Available at http://www.saigon.com/~nike/apjun22.html/ Retrieved June 25, 1997.

Strange, S. (1988). *States and markets.* London: Pinter.

Straubhaar, J. (1991). Beyond media imperialism: Asymmetrical interdependence and cultural proximity. *Critical Studies in Mass Communication* 8:39–-59.

Sunday Vanguard (2000, July 10). The amalgamation of Nigeria was a fraud—Akinjide. *Sunday Vanguard.* [Online]. Available at http://www.vanguard.com/ Retrieved July 12, 2000.

Sussman, G. (1997). *Communication, technology and politics in the information age.* Thousand Oaks, CA: Sage.

Tansey, R., & M. Hyman (1994). Dependency theory and the effects of advertising by foreign based multinational corporations in Latin America. *Journal of Advertising* 23(1):27–41.

Tantavichien, A. (1989). *The role of advertising in Thailand's national development.* [Unpublished] California State University, Fresno.

Taylor, M. (2000). Toward a public relations approach for nation building. *Journal of Public Relations Research* 12:178–-210.

Taylor, R., E. Hoy, & M. Grubbs (1996). How French advertising professionals develop creative strategy. *Journal of Advertising* 25(1):1–14.

The Guardian (1999, May 11). World bank sells Africa's potential to European investors. [Online]. Available at http://www.ngrgurardiannews.com/ Retrieved May 12, 1999.

The Guardian Online (2001, April 19). 8,000-year-old canoe to get own museum. [Online]. Available at http://www.ngrguardiannews.com. Retrieved April 10, 2001.

The Guardian Online (2001, Aug. 13). Nigeria is world's 10th populous nation, says report. [Online]. Available at http://www.ngrguadian.com/.Retrieved Aug. 15, 2001.

The Indian Express Newspaper (Bombay) Ltd., *The Financial Express*, and Reuters (1997, June 26). US cigarette makers in search of new markets. [Online]. Available at http://www.expressindia.com/Retrieved June 26, 1997.

ThisDay (1998, Dec. 12). APCON is over-regulating. *Adelaja*, p. 8.

Thussu, D. (2000). *International communication: Continuity and change.* London: Arnold.

Tsao, J. (1996). Advertising in Taiwan: Sociopolitical changes and multinational impact. In K. Frith (ed.), *Advertising in Asia: communication, culture and consumption* (pp. 103–114). Ames: Iowa State University Press.

Uche, L. (1988). Mass communication and cultural Identity: The unresolved issue of national sovereignty and cultural autonomy in the wake of new communication technologies. *Africa Media Review* 3(1):83–120.

Uche, L. (1994). Some reflections on the dependency theory. *Africa Media Review* 8(2):39–55.

Uche, L. (1997, Sept. 8–10). The economic and emancipative potentials of the information superhighway regime for Africa south of the Sahara. Paper presented at the Regional workshop on media ownership and control in West and Central Africa, Yaounde, Cameroon.

United Nations/Economic Commission for Africa (1998). United Nations/Economic Commission for Africa (1998, Feb. 5). *Special initiatives on Africa—A framework agenda for building and utilizing critical parties in Africa—Part II.* [Online]. Available at http://www.undp.org/ Retrieved March 10, 2001.

Vande Berg, L., L. Wenner, & B. Gronbeck (1998). *Critical approaches to television.* Boston: Houghton Mifflin.

Vanguard (1999, Nov. 11). *Marketing is a tool for economic development—Tunde Ojo.* [Online]. Available at http://www.afbis.com.vanguard/fp212799.html This date reflect the date of retrieval, not publication. Date of publication is unstated in online printout.

Vanguard (2000, Aug. 28). Nigeria's economy needs diversification—Clinton. [Online]. httpl/www.vanguardngr.com/Retrieved Aug. 28, 2000.

Vanguard (2000, Feb. 14). AAPN set to increase participation in government. [Online]. httpl/www.vanguardngr.com/Retrieved Feb. 15, 2000.

Vanguard (2000, Feb. 21). FG's annual ad-expenditure totals N10 million. [Online]. Available at http://www.vanguardngr.com/ Retrieved Feb. 25, 2000.

Vanguard (2006, Feb. 2006a), Bad leadership and the curse of the Nigerian nation, by Akinjide. [Online]. Available at http://www.vanguardngr.com/ Retrieved Feb. 21, 2006.

Vanguard (2006, Feb. 2006b), Nigerian leaders fail to take responsibilities—Akunyili. Available at *http://www.vanguardngr.com/* Retrieved Feb. 21, 2006.

Wacieni, K. (1996). False hope. *Harvard International Review* 18(4):42–73.

Ward, H. (1989). *African development reconsidered: New perspectives from the continent.* New York: A Phelps-Stokes Publication.

Wells, A. (1972). Picture-tube imperialism: The impact of US television on Latin America America. Maryknoll, NY: Orbis Books

Wells, A. (1994). *Picture tube imperialism? The impact of US television on Latin America.* New York: Orbis.

Wells, W., J. Burnett, & S. Moriarty (1992). *Advertising: Principles and practices* (2nd ed.). Englewood Cliffs, NJ: Prentice Hall.

Whetmore, E. (1995). *Media America, mediaworld: Form, content, and consequence of mass communication.* Belmont, CA: Wadsworth.

Wimmer, R., & J. Dominick (1994). *Mass media research: An introduction* (4th ed.). Belmont, CA: Wadsworth.

Woods, B (1993). *Communication, technology and the development of people.* London: Routledge.

Yushikiavitshus, H. (1994). Quoted in A. de Beer, F. Kasoma, E. Megwa, & E. Steyn (1995). Sub-Saharan Africa. In J. Merrill (ed.), *Global journalism: Survey of international communication* (3rd ed., pp. 209–268). White Plains, NY: Longman.

Zandpour, F., V. Campos, J. Catalano, C. Chang, Y. Cho, R. Hoobyar, H.-F. Jiang, M.-C. Lin, S. Madrid, P. Scheideler, & S. Osborn (1994). Global outreach and local touch: Achieving fitness in TV advertising. *Journal of Advertising Research* 34(5):35–63.

Ziegler, D., & M. Asante (1992). *Thunder and silence: The mass media in Africa.* Trenton, NJ: Africa World Press.

Index